Cary Kassebaum

This book belongs to
Wendy Witt

Read by:
Wendy - Oct 2019

DEDICATION

My partner in life, Hazel
Michael and Lancelot – who would have ever thought
Allan and David, always steadfast

PREFACE

I spent almost 30 years in the Foreign Service of the United States. Unlike the usual Foreign Service career, I changed agencies frequently to the point that, when I retired, it was unclear from which agency I retired.

I've been involved in five wars. The Vietnam War is now over thirty years ago. My role in the anti-narcotics wars in Colombia in the 70's and Peru in the late 80's, the efforts to bring down the Communist government in Ethiopia in 1984 and the U. S. support for Chad in its war with Libya in the early 90's reflect the Cold War atmosphere of the times. I'm not James Bond or even his little brother. I never shot at anybody (although I am sorry to say that I have sent others to do it for me). I did have a talent for getting shot at. Except for the refugee posts – Singapore, Hong Kong and the Philippines – I managed to have bullets fly my direction in every other post. My career spanned from 1966 to 1995. It was a time before the world became as homogenized as it is today with instant communications, internet and television. I saw and lived with people only beginning to change from static cultures little different from centuries earlier. It was a privilege. The world will continue to change and in a few decades those of us who have lived in the era covered by this book will be gone. This is my attempt to keep a small part of it from disappearing.

The Early Years

I was born on a cold day – the twelfth of December, 1944 – in the small town of Beatrice, Nebraska. Beatrice is – and was – a small town of about 12,000. It is surrounded by miles of corn fields and crisscrossed with tree-lined streams and rivers. The Blue River passes through the town giving people a place to fish and for kids to swim. The young people tend to move out because there isn't a lot of work but they are replaced by older folks from the rural areas who retire. The population hasn't changed in 60 years. It is small enough that a 15 minute walk will take you almost anywhere and lots of people know each other. All it needs is Opie and Aunt Bee. Both of my parents grew up in Beatrice, met in high school and fell in love.

My father, Leslie, really never knew his father, Frank, even though his father died in 1932 when Father was 11 years old. Frank had tuberculosis. It developed around the time my father was born. In the 1920s,

TB was considered to be highly contagious. His father stayed in a back bedroom and the children were never allowed to enter the room or talk with him. His food was carried in and the dishes boiled afterward. Leslie didn't know Frank and never did anything with his father. When it was clear that Frank had reached the end, the family gathered for one photo with the children standing as close to Frank as they had ever been. My father is the youngest boy on the left. When my grandfather Kassebaum died in 1932 at the beginning of the Depression, all of his children except my father dropped out of school to help support the family. As a result my father was the only child in his family to finish high school. After graduation he joined the Army to do his part in World War II and was sent to California for training as a pilot.

My mother, Emma Applegarth, was the oldest of eight children her mother produced. Her mother, Alice Blanche Byrd, married 24 year old William Walter Applegarth when she was only 15. Walter had diabetes, an untreatable disease at the time. Walter died at the age of 27 leaving my mother, age three, my mother's year old sister, Louise, and an 18 year old widow. My mother's version of her childhood was that she was left with her grandmother and an aunt and uncle to be raised. Others in the family say that her grandmother, a strong willed woman, made it clear that little Emma would stay with or without Blanche's permission. Blanche took sister Louise and began work as a housekeeper for a much older man with two teenage sons.

They married and divorced (or perhaps not – neither is clear). After producing 6 more children, she abandoned them all and went on to have a string of lovers. There also is some debate over her marriage status to these later ventures. She (apparently) married the last of these men when she was about 40 years old and stayed with him for over 40 years. They later lived in Florida with my mother's sister, Louise, until they died in their 80s.

Whatever the truth, my mother remained bitter and angry toward her mother – as did the other 6 children. I saw my grandmother a few times as a child only because she lived next door to the aunt and uncle that raised Emma.

My mother's story – probably partly true – is that she bought a one-way train ticket to San Francisco to visit my father while he was in pilot training and announced to my father that he had better marry her since she did not have the money to return home. Air Cadets were not allowed to marry but my father somehow got permission. They were married in May of 1943. Like thousands of others during the war, they realized that my father might not return. Perhaps grasping at immortality, he left my mother pregnant before he shipped overseas. He did return and I was not one of the thousands of children who never knew their fathers.

Pregnant Mother returned to Beatrice. Soon my 20 year old mother went with her grandmother to the Lutheran Hospital for my birth. I have the bill for my mother's seven day hospital stay - $49.50. This included a $1.00 charge for circumcision. I hate to think that my surgery was considered that minor. Father was in England with the 8th Army Air Force flying B-17s against the Germans and was notified of the arrival of his son by a telegram that I still have. World War II was in its last days with Germany pressed ever tighter between the British and American forces on the west and the Russians on the east. The fighting would be more intense as the Germans were compressed back into their own country.

Let me take you back to the 1940s. Now sit down for this – no plastic. No computers, cell phones, televisions, home air conditioning or portable music. There was no such thing as a credit card, fast food or disposable cups, plates or boxes. Airplanes had propellers, cars were 7 feet high. There were no new cars since production stopped to support the war. The Midwest was blanketed with thousands of small towns like Beatrice, many are now long abandoned. Many of these small towns had no electricity or central water systems. Less than half the people of the United States – the world's most advanced country – had telephones in their homes. More people lived on farms than in the cities, graduating from high school was an accomplishment shared by little more than half of the young people. Franklin Roosevelt was president, as he had been for the last 13 years. The country and the world had survived the worst economic depression in history. The need for massive workforces to support the war finally brought some prosperity to the average person. It also brought women into the workforce for the first time. The war devastated huge areas of Europe, Asia, Russia and North Africa. The United States was fortunate. The Japanese bombed Pearl Harbor, temporarily occupied a few small uninhabited Aleutian Islands and, in a final gasp of desperation, launched some balloons from a submarine that set fire to a few trees in Oregon. Otherwise the nation remained undamaged.

By my first birthday, Franklin Roosevelt was dead, the Germans surrendered and the Japanese, hit by the first atomic bomb at Hiroshima but only convinced by the second at Nagasaki, signed an unconditional surrender in Tokyo Harbor. The process of releasing several million American soldiers was not an easy one. The massive war industry shut down with the loss of millions of jobs. The prosperity of wartime salaries and savings fueled a new market for goods and services but business had not caught up with the change. To ease the return, the government created programs for returning soldiers to go off to college.

My father returned in 1945. With the war not quite over, the three of us lived near military bases in California, New Mexico, Texas and then California again while my father helped to train more pilots. When the war finally did end, my father had few choices. He could return to Nebraska with no certainty of work. The college programs did not supply enough money to support a wife and child. He decided to stay in the military. The military demobilized millions but recognized that he was a skilled pilot and kept him.

My earliest memories are in San Francisco. My father retrained to fly large cargo planes. My mother worked in a small beauty salon. (For some mysterious reason, she later swore she never worked a day in her life.) The salon was in a private home and I wandered the back yard and through the owner's greenhouse while she  worked. My father was often gone. He flew to Hawaii and Japan and was once assigned to fly a U.S. supplied plane for the King of Thailand. On his first day in Thailand he went exploring Bangkok in an Army Jeep. Warned of theft, he chained the steering wheel of the Jeep to a tree while he dined in a nearby restaurant. When he returned the steering wheel was still chained to the tree – the rest of the vehicle gone. After a few days in Bangkok, he sat in the plane awaiting the King to arrive

 to fly to some upcountry town. On the way to the airport the King was assassinated. Our government

withdrew the plane and crew, ending what could have been an exciting assignment.

We lived in several places near San Francisco. The earliest that I remember was a small second floor place with an outside staircase. I became an accomplished escape artist. It was too hot in the California weather to sleep with the wooden door shut and I was good at figuring out how to unlatch the screen door. As an early riser, I liked to escape and cruise the neighbor's back doors for their milk deliveries. In those days, unhomogenized milk was delivered in the early morning and left at the door in glass bottles. I liked to pull off the paper cap and suck off the cream. I often got busted but the neighbors were kind. According to my mother, I usually made my route in a wet diaper that might disappear along the way.

Later we lived in a small wooden house. Father and Mother bought a black cocker spaniel puppy. Little boys and little puppies do not mix well and they had to get rid of it before I loved it to death. I had a tricycle and the world expanded as I peddled around the neighborhood.

Another early memory is driving from Beatrice to San Francisco on Route 66 in a 1936 Ford coupe, along with my mother's great-aunt Maggie. Aunt Maggie was old and old school, heavily dressed in billowing black. Since this car had only one seat (It's the car seen on the previous pages.), I was relegated to spending most of the trip slowly baking on the package shelf. Fortunately for me, Maggie could only do about 20 miles before needing a trip to the bushes and giving me a break. The trip took days. On another trip back to San Francisco from Beatrice (I have no recollection of how we got to Beatrice.) my mother and I took the train. Somewhere in Colorado the snow covered the tracks and the train was trapped for a day or two. Nicely heated and with plenty of food, I played with my wooden blocks in the rear observation car on the thick carpet with scattered big leather easy chairs.

In 1947 my mother delivered a stillborn daughter who is buried in a military cemetery within sight of the Golden Gate Bridge. Strangely the government supplied headstone reads "Daughter of Lt. Leslie Kassebaum" as if my mother was not involved.

In 1948 Father was transferred to Hickam Field in Honolulu, Hawaii. We lived in a two story home at the end of a U-shaped complex of twelve townhouses. We arrived in the summer and there were loads of other kids for me to play with. When the school year began in September there suddenly were no other kids in the neighborhood. I must have driven my mother crazy before she took me to the school and demanded that I be enrolled in kindergarten. I was three and the lower age limit was five. I had a highly intelligent mother who did not believe in baby talk. I sounded older in spite of my size. I'm sure that the school thought it easier to deal with a three year old than my mother and reluctantly placed me in class. The original plan was for me to go to kindergarten for two years and start the First Grade when I was five – still a year under the limit. At the end of the school year, no doubt fearing my return, the kindergarten teacher strongly recommended to the school and my parents that I go on to the First Grade. The picture is the first day of Grade One. I loved school and the age difference had no impact – for a while. This rippled through my entire school career, a first-grader at 4, junior high at 10 and high school at 12. The school was near the beach, had only a roof and walls at each end of each class with four foot open partitions on the sides. The smell of the sea, flowers and pineapple fields wafted

through the rooms. Most of the boys, and some of the girls, went to school shirtless and shoeless. It was heaven. Since I spent those years mostly shoeless and shirtless even in school, I still hate shoes.

Hawaii, in the 1940's, was a very different place from today. Commercial airlines could only carry passengers on the 2,200 miles trip to the islands by seaplane. They were luxurious but expensive and there were only three flights a week. An occasional cruise ship appeared but tourists were few and infrequent. The only notable hotel was the Royal Hawaiian on Waikiki Beach. Honolulu was small, quiet and unhurried. In general the Chinese and Japanese ran small shops and restaurants while the Filipinos and Koreans worked the surrounding sugar and pineapple fields. There was little traffic or noise. It had a small town feel to it. Because the population was mostly Asian many of them were intrigued by my then white hair. Unlike today, we ran free in the neighborhoods and beaches unafraid of child molesters or kidnappers.

We had a very large tree in our yard and I liked to climb high up to the top. My best friend is Mike. For some strange reason his mother insists that he always wear shoes and he can't climb this tree wearing them. Sometimes he cheated when his mother wasn't watching but he chickened out at the first limb. Sometimes I liked to jam a book into the back of my shorts, climb the tree and read.

Father bought a Cushman scooter. It had three wheels and a large box on the front. He also bought a German Weimeraner dog. Herman and I took many rides in the box around the base and to the beach. Herman outweighed me by a lot but put up with me walking him on a leash – most of the time. If he spied a cat all bets were off and he several times drug me on my stomach around the neighborhood in pursuit. Well, Mother did say, "Don't let go!" Shirtless, I'm surprised my navel isn't now

on one knee or the other.

Father has regular hours for a change. He flies to Japan, stays for a day and flies home so that he is gone three days and home for two. For the first time he is regularly present. We were a young family. My father and mother were still in their early 20's. I wasn't spoiled or overindulged (well, not much) but I did benefit from a lot of undivided attention. We trooped off to the beach, explored the sugarcane and pineapple fields and visited the Pali. The Pali is the top of a breech between two volcanoes in Oahu. The winds from the east are funneled up the valley and pass through the Pali at 50 to 70 mph. Reached by a single lane road now long closed, the top was great fun as I clung to my father's hand to avoid (I thought) sailing off in the wind over the valley to land in the bay below. On other days, my father and I went fishing off the docks of Pearl Harbor or to "Wahini Kapu," ("No Women Allowed" in Hawaiian). An annex to the Officer's Club, Wahini Kapu was a grass hut with a bar and pool table that sat right on the beach. While Father had a beer with his friends, I played in the sand and poked around in the coconut trees, proud of the fact that I was in a place my mother could not go.

I must have been about four years old when my father first took me fishing. We sat on the docks of Pearl Harbor. Something tugged my line and I pulled it up very slowly as my father instructed. At the end of the line were two crabs fighting over the bait. When I lowered them to the dock they released their hold and scuttled toward me. With a scream, I dropped the pole and ran off down the dock. I have never enjoyed fishing from that time on.

In 1950 automobile manufacturers finally restored full production of cars. My father bought a black 1950 Buick, the first new car they owned. A few years later, it would be the first car I ever drove. It cost a whopping $2,200, almost a year's salary for my father. (Years later we found my father's W-2 form for 1948. He earned $2,400 that year.) This huge beast replaced an even bigger 1938 Buick that my father bought when

 we arrived in Honolulu. My mother hated that '38. Once the floor standard-shift lever came out in her hand in the middle of traffic. We drove home in second gear in a cloud of burning clutch. When it baulked at starting, my father attempted to fix it himself. Even at six feet, his legs were in the air and his head deep in the engine compartment

when it decided it would now cooperate. The engine started. We watched as he extricated himself from the bowels of the engine and chased the slowly moving empty car down the street.

On its first trip to the beach where the Army had some cabins, the '50 Buick rolled onto the sandy beach road. About 10 inches from the end of the pavement, it majestically went down like the Titanic in the sand to the level of the doors. Manufactured without plastic or aluminum, with sheet metal much thicker and heavier than today, it probably weighed 6,000 lbs. It took a 2 ½ ton Army tow truck to pull it free. One of my first jobs was to floss the chrome teeth of this monster. My smaller hands could get the chrome polish between those teeth. It took a whole bottle of chrome polish each time. The

grill alone weighed more than a Volkswagen. They drove this thing until 1957 when they traded it in for another new car. My father failed to mention at trade-in that my mother had caused the right front fender to be replaced five times.

We often made trips to the beach cabins with other families.

The Blankenships had a daughter my age – "Sticky Vicky". Vicky loved oranges and usually had sticky hands that left residue on everything she touched. I hated oranges for years. My mother taught me to swim on one of these trips but I was not allowed to go into the water alone without a small life jacket. Unsinkable, I often paddled far out to the anchored sailboats in the bay. Father had a one-man inflatable life raft that he and his friends would fill with beer and haul out to one of these sailboats. They would trespass on the boats, spending the afternoon talking and letting me float around. Probably deliberately, they never remembered to bring anything for me to drink. Thirst would drive me back to the beach to leave them in peace.

My father did disappear for some months in the late 1940's. The Russians blockaded Berlin and the U.S. responded with the Berlin Airlift. He flew several flights a day between England and Berlin to carry supplies to keep the city functioning. So dense was the air traffic that if a pilot missed his approach to the runway he returned to England with his cargo to refuel and try again. He found himself flying to save the same city that he had bombed a few years earlier. When Stalin gave up the blockade he returned to Hawaii.

When the Korean War heated up around 1950, my father stopped the regular flights to Japan and began flying hospital planes between Korea and Hawaii to bring back the wounded for medical treatment. The plane's crew included several nurses and one of my father's favorite stories involved a nurse who augmented her attributes with some sort of pneumatic falsies that grew larger as the plane gained altitude.

In 1950 my mother had another miscarriage. My parents always wanted three children but this event made them give up the idea for several years. The problem was the then unsolvable problem of the RH factor. My father was RH positive and my mother RH negative. It has no effect on the first child but leaves antibodies in the mother that causes a reaction in many successive pregnancies. I was nine years old before medical advances solved the problem.

History lesson

Gen. Charles MacArthur was one of the country's most brilliant soldiers. First in his West Point class, military governor of the Philippines (his aide was an unknown Major Dwight Eisenhower), Supreme Allied Commander in Asia during WW II and governor of Japan after the war. He also was arrogant and had an enormous ego. When Communist North Korea invaded South Korea he was appointed Commander of the United Nations forces ordered to push back the invasion. MacArthur succeeded in pushing the Communists back to the Chinese border. His orders from President Truman were clear - in no case cross the Chinese border in pursuit of the enemy. MacArthur was disdainful of President Truman, privately calling him the "Little Corporal" in reference to Truman's service in WW I. MacArthur, believing the pursuit of the Communist troops was necessary for victory, ignored this order and sent probes across the border. As Truman feared, China responded by sending hundreds of thousands of troops into the battle and, in a short time, the UN forces were pushed back into a small pocket on the South Korean coast. This nearly lost the war.

President Truman in April 1951 flew through Hawaii to Midway Island to meet MacArthur. MacArthur ordered his pilot to circle the island until after Truman landed so that the press would see the President waiting for him. Truman got on the radio and ordered MacArthur's pilot to land immediately. They met and Truman fired MacArthur. Truman later said, "I didn't fire him because he was a dumb son of a bitch – which he was. I fired him because he disobeyed the Commander-In-Chief." It was one of the most unpopular decisions of his administration. The enormously popular MacArthur returned to the States to ticker tape parades and cheering crowds, retired and decided to run for President. Said Truman, "In six months nobody will remember this guy." Truman was correct. (end)

As Truman flew back to Washington, his plane stopped at Hickam Field to refuel and be serviced. Father took me down to the small terminal at the airfield to see the President. There was a small crowd of perhaps thirty people since the stop was neither publicized nor was the base open to the public. Father put me on his shoulders to that I could see. Truman entered, broke out into a big smile and began to circulate through the small crowd shaking hands. He reached us, shook Father's hand and then reached up and shook my dangling bare foot. Many people have shaken the hand of the President. I doubt that many can say that the President of the United States shook their bare foot.

Hawaii was a great place to be a kid. I spent days on the beach, wandered the neighborhood barefoot and played with friends of every race and background. The airbase had a large number of local contractors of diverse backgrounds so that many of my playmates were Japanese, Chinese, Filipino, Black, Hawaiian and so on. My mother and father took me everywhere with them during the day. The weather was perfect, even the rain was warm. My parents were in their mid 20's, athletic and social. I have only fond memories of Hawaii.

Texas

We left Hawaii in 1953 when I was 9 years old. It left me forever hooked on the warm soft air of the tropics. Father was transferred to San Antonio, Texas, first to Kelly Air Force Base and then Brooks Field. Shortly after we arrived my mother gave birth to my sister Nina. She arrived months early and weighing only 2 lbs. 2 oz. Children were banned from the hospital and I never actually saw her until 1954 because she was kept in the hospital until she weighed 6 ½ lbs.

Texas was my introduction to segregation, something that did not exist in Hawaii. President Truman had integrated the military back in 1948. In Hawaii there was no segregation on or off the bases. My father and I were walking in a park and I noticed that there were two water fountains to drink from – one marked "White" and the other "Colored". Father had a difficult time explaining this. It struck both of us as stupid but he needed me to know that it was equally stupid to talk about it with most of the local people. I didn't care much for Texas. On the first day of school, I went off to Grade 6 in new clothes – shirt, shoes and shorts. I was immediately sent home. I lost the battle over shirt and shoes as I knew I would. Neither my mother nor I knew that the school required long pants and collared shirts that buttoned in the very humid, hot 100+ degree weather – in an un-air-conditioned school! Students sweltered in the heat, windows open and a few ceiling fans doing little. For much of the year we all sat dripping and lethargic. On really hot days recess would be canceled because there was no shade on the playground.

 After we lived for a few months in a duplex, we moved to a rented house on Mink Drive. When I came home from school one day, an upright piano had been delivered and installed in the living room. Neither my father nor my mother played – a bad sign. I was expected to learn how to play this thing and was enrolled for the next four years in private lessons from several piano teachers. I hated it and had little aptitude for it but eventually learned to read music and pound out the right keys. Playing the right notes in the right order without rhythm, cadence or feeling is not music. I had one teacher – an old woman – who could play anything but only in 4-4 time. She managed to make "You Ain't Nothin' But a Hound Dog" into a waltz. No matter what she played it came out as a waltz and this was the woman who was going to teach me.

Mother, who'd already torn the front fender off the Buick on several occasions, scored her biggest accident with this car by almost destroying the rented house on Mink Drive. This house was covered in fieldstone – large chunks of irregularly shaped stones stacked and cemented to form the outer walls. Arriving home one day after school, she just missed the opening of the garage and caught the edge of the front bumper on the frame of the garage door. In slow motion the entire front of the house fell forward onto lawn where they came apart and rolled in all directions. The stones over the garage door crashed onto the hood of the car. The landlord, who conveniently lived next door, came running out on the verge of a coronary. His rented house was now a tar-paper shack. It took a crew of men about ten days to reassemble the stones that only fit together in one way. They hauled them about ("Nope – not here") until they figured out the pattern and could reattach them to the house. It wasn't a surprise when we moved shortly afterward. She also hit a lawyer – good move – and a light in a parking lot. When she hit a boy on a bicycle (no harm done) her driving improved for a short time.

We bought a bulldog named "Spike," another dog that weighed more than I. Spike loved people and kids but hated other animals. I began to play musical schools (Better than the piano, I might add). I started at a school near the duplex then switched to another when we moved to the rented house. I finished Grade Six and moved to a Junior High School. Then we moved again and I changed schools again. By the Seventh Grade I had attended six schools. Around 1955 my father bought his first house at 143 Tipperary Street in San Antonio. Brand new, it cost $12,500. It had four bedrooms. Sister Lisa arrived in 1955 to make this a full house. Each room had a gas jet for small heaters, but no air conditioning. Nina was crawling by this time and turned on these jets several times. It is a wonder that the house never exploded into a ball of fire. Father added a garage at the rear and later bought one of the first portable window air conditioners. This "portable" took two men to lift and install and stuck so far out into the driveway that the car had to drive off into the grass to pass it. When turned on, it dimmed all the

 lights in the house for a moment and did little more than cool the living room. On really hot days I would lie on the cool linoleum floor of the living room and read. Later, our first television was added. This huge cabinet was filled with dozens of hot glass tubes that canceled out much of the work of the air conditioner. The television frequently stopped working. Father and I numbered the tubes so that we could remove all of them – you never knew which one failed – and cart them off to a small store nearby that had a tube tester. We would test each one. Sometimes more than one failed so we would have to test all of them. Father would buy a replacement for the bad tubes, we'd go home and reinstall all of them into the numbered sockets and hope it worked for a while longer. Think of it as the video game of 1957.

My mother and father decided to join a church. My father never mentioned attending church as a child but my mother was often taken to the Methodist Church in Beatrice by her grandmother. They found a small Methodist church not far from the house and we began to attend regularly. I was sent to Sunday School as well. It didn't last. The minister was a young man who gave quiet sermons. After a few months he announced that he had cancer and would be replaced by another older minister. We didn't see the younger minister for a while until they announced his funeral service. Not long after that the older minister had a heart attack and died. We stopped attending and I left with the impression that religion wasn't very good for your health.

My last brush with religion occurred when one of the neighbors invited my mother to attend church with her. I don't know what possessed her to accept but she drug me off with her. Neither of us knew they were Holy Rollers. At first I was frightened by the sight of adults rolling on the floor, bawling their eyes out and babbling in incomprehensible tongues. Mother whispered, "They are supposed to do that." We both got a case of the giggles. We were not invited back.

When I was 11 I started delivering the morning newspaper to about 60 homes nearby. I earned a profit of 50 cents per month for each home, in theory at least. I'd get up at 5 A.M. to wrap the papers and deliver them by bicycle before school. Once a month in the afternoons I had to collect from the customers. Some took three or four visits to squeeze out the money. Some moved without paying. One woman flat told me she would not pay. I took the losses for those who did not pay. I was encouraged to quit after about six months because we could not go anywhere and I wasn't making much money.

Two doors down from us lived Corbett. Corbett was my age, although he went to a different school, and lived in a small house with a lot of brothers and sisters. He and his brothers lived in a small bedroom with two sets of bunk beds. Corbett and I became good after-school friends and the two of us spent hours in the open dusty fields at both ends of the street. We built dirt forts, extensive highways for toy trucks and cars, marble mazes and usually came home dirty and sweaty. Corbett liked to stay overnight at our house, away from the crowded house he lived in. His family had a poor dog tied in the back yard that received little attention. One afternoon, as we played in his backyard, the dog bit me.

His father refused to have the dog tested for rabies and I had to get the full rabies treatment of the time — 12 shots in the stomach. They were very painful. My father finally called the police to get the dog tested. After that, Corbett was not allowed to see me.

In 1956 we had a bad scare about my father. He developed nephritis and spent over a month in the hospital. There was no cure and dialysis or transplants had yet to come. At first my mother worried that he might die from the disease. This was not discussed with me. Later, as he improved, he was afraid that he would lose his flight status and perhaps his career. During his hospital stay my mother spent every evening with him while I looked after three year old Nina and baby Lisa. This cured me of any future desire for babies. It defied all logic that more came out of these two than went in. (Sorry, Sis!) He eventually recovered enough to go back to work and, later, obtained a waiver to fly. Much more serious kidney problems would develop years later.

My age wasn't a problem through grade school. There were always kids my age around the school in the lower grades. However, when I went off to Junior High it was different. Most 7th graders were 13 years old and I was 10. I always did very well in school and it brought me a certain amount of respect from classmates. I was treated well by the others but rarely chosen as a friend. While most of the other boys were dealing with the mysteries of adolescence I didn't have a clue what their world was about. They were mooning over the girls in the class and I was still at the "girls are icky" stage. I coped with it all by being funny and smart and it earned me some acceptance. I was high on the approach-avoidance scale. When somebody needed a partner for a school project, I was a good bet. If they needed help with homework, few wanted to be seen getting it from a 10 year old. With the three moves and four schools in five years, I had no network of other friends. I withdrew into books, science and math. Forget sports – I was even small for age 10. Most organized sports for kids were at the schools and kids my size and age were back in the elementary schools. Overall, I found Texas to be a lonely place. I don't look back on Texas with many fond memories. Hot, dusty, segregated and bigoted.

Even 60 years later, I see that this age thing dominated my childhood in and out of school. At 7 I talked and often had the interests of a 10 year old and many adults thought I was some sort of exceptional child. I was not, of course, but learned to 'give them what they wanted' with an advanced vocabulary

 from my parents. My mother gave me a section of the Reader's Digest that each month listed commonly misunderstood words.

I was expected to use them properly. Emotionally I was still a 7 year old but I didn't fit there either. While many 7 year olds were learning to read and add and subtract, I read parts of the newspaper and did long division. Seven year olds bored me and 10 year olds mystified me. From moment to moment, I fit anywhere or nowhere.

I never discussed this with my mother and father. They were

proud of my accomplishments and I saw no solutions. Even I didn't want to drop back in school. As an only child with very social parents, I spent a lot of time with adults. Usually I could charm them. Kids were much tougher and so I eventually preferred to spend my time with adults. As I now look back on it, I think I often just did not know how to be a kid.

Newfoundland

In 1957 Father was transferred to Harmon Air Force Base in Stephensville, Newfoundland. The best part of the move? That  the damned piano was left behind. Fortunately for me pianos do not ship well and there were no piano tuners in Newfoundland. It was my first exposure to prolonged cold weather and I didn't like it at all. School promised to be a definite improvement. I was a 12 year old 9th grader in high school. Because military people have the option of retiring at a relatively young age, military bases usually don't have many teenagers. At Harmon the junior and senior high schools were combined for the small number of students. My first year there the school was in an un-insulated wooden building heated by oil-fired pot belly stoves in the middle of the class. Too close and you melted, too far and you froze. Mondays were the worst. The building sat unheated over the weekend and often there was ice and frost inside. But at least I would have other kids my age in the school in the junior high section and we all lived in a small housing area so that I would see them after school as well.

This all sounded good but I turned out to be wrong. Grade nine became the worst year yet. For once we moved during the school summer break. I enrolled in the new school as soon as we arrived. September arrived and I went off for the first day of school. The home room teacher – a dark, flabby woman with hair on her upper lip that was the envy of the 15 year old boys who sat in front of her – was a horror. She was only there for a few months and I have successfully blotted out her name from memory. When the bell rang, she stood and immediately zeroed in on me.

"This is the ninth grade. Are you in the right room?"

"Yes," I sighed.

"What's your name?" I told her, she scanned a list, found my name and seemed satisfied.

"Just how old are you?" she asked.

"Twelve." Every kid in the class swiveled around to look at me. Naturally I felt even smaller and younger now. There were a few kids who had not jumped in height yet so I guess they could deal with little but not with twelve.

There were about 20 14 to 16 year old kids in the ninth grade. In military schools there is usually a lot of turnover but most of this class stayed together for the next three years. I give these kids credit – I cannot recall ever being teased about size or age.

Kids in their middle teens are not known for sensitivity but this group proved to be OK. I got along well with all of them in school but, of course, I ceased to exist when the bell rang at the end of the day.

I sat next to Joe Jedrakowski. Joe was probably 16. He worked very hard in school with very mediocre results. I liked history and could usually describe historical events and the effects they had. Joe thought this was borderline amazing. Soon, whenever he saw me coming he would announce, "Here comes the Walking Encyclopedia." He wasn't being sarcastic and, for awhile, I got stuck with that. It doesn't exactly roll off the tongue so it eventually died out.

The one class I absolutely hated was Physical Education. Three times a week all the high school boys bundled up and walked about a block to the Base Gymnasium. There was almost always too much snow and much too cold to do anything outside. The junior high kids were on a different schedule. The gym consisted of a large basketball court (oh, great!), showers and dressing rooms and little else. There I was with a group of 15 to 18 year olds on a basketball court. Even some of the boys in my ninth grade class were six feet tall. I was about 4' 6" and maybe 70 lbs. Height had never been an issue with me; I was used to being a few inches shorter than most of the people in my class. At this point, some of these kids were 18 inches taller than me. With the exception of some climbing ropes – I was light and

agile – I feared for my life in this class. At least the PE teacher didn't put me into the basketball games. One of the first activities we tried was dodge ball. I actually wasn't too bad at this because I was a small target and fairly quick. We used a basketball that bounced off those who didn't 'dodge' fast enough. Eventually, some kid did hit me. It knocked me about three feet flat on my back. As I laid there dazed with blood streaming out of the back of my head, the poor kid who threw the ball thought he had killed me. For a moment I thought he might be right.

At the end of this 1 ½ hour torture session there were mandatory communal showers. The less said about that, the better. Eventually, thanks to early puberty, at least that wasn't too bad.

Eventually the PE teacher and I reached an unspoken agreement. I spent a lot of time moving from one activity to another without actually joining them. He pretended to not notice. I think this was the only "C" grade I received in school. I took it and was glad.

My social life was an absolute zero. The base had a Teen Club where my classmates could hang out, listen to music, dance and so on. It had a snack bar with a de facto adult supervisor. *("Sorry. You're too young.")* The junior high part of the school also held school parties and dances. *("Sorry. No high school boys.")* I couldn't win.My second year the base converted a barracks into a decent high school with heat that worked and classrooms that looked like a school. During the summer between 9th and 10th grades a growth spurt kicked in and I grew about 8 inches. During this process I slept most of the time and my joints hurt all of the time. I was finally the same size as some of the other boys in my classes. Like every other boy who ever lived, I had discovered the delights of a newly developed body, although for some months I just knew that other boys didn't do any of this. My father would have left the country before he would have discussed anything like this with me. At school we boys traded information – and misinformation - and convinced each other that we were all just fine. Now I had some clue about the seemingly strange behavior of other kids.

Until this growth spurt I usually was seated in the front row of the class because it was difficult for me to see over or around bigger classmates. My 10th grade English teacher was Miss Liebowitz. She was in her 20's and had enormous breasts that the boys found enormously interesting. She sat me near the back of the class *("Great. Now I'm out of the front row.").* After a week or so, she sent me home with a note asking my parents to meet with her. When she gave me this note I asked if I had done something wrong. She told me not to worry but that she did need to talk with my parents.

Instead of meeting her at the school, my mother invited my teacher for dinner – every kid's nightmare. She came and dinner went well until she announced that she thought I had a problem. *(Oh, God! What? Staring at her boobs? All the boys did that.)* Miss Liebowitz thought that I had poor eyesight! She said she noticed that I squinted at the blackboard. Often that wasn't exactly what I was squinting at but she didn't' bring that up.

After school the next day, my mother hauled me off to the base hospital and the optometrist. Sure enough, I was nearsighted and needed glasses. I thought this was nonsense but the doctor made me agree to at least try them out. It took a week to make them in the only thing available, the fashionable military issue frames. When they arrived, Mother more or less dragged me back to the hospital to get them. The doctor fiddled and bent them until they fit, placed them on my head and told me to go look out the window. I did and thought, *"Holy Crap! Is this what other people see?"* Brown sticks with green cones on top turned into pine trees. Black blobs in the sky turned into birds. I was amazed at the difference. I'd no idea that other people could see this clearly.

I was a bit self-conscious the next day at school but soon

discovered that my friends didn't really care. After that I only took them off to read or to sleep. Unfortunately my eyesight got progressively worse at a rapid pace. I needed a new prescription every few months and I soon could only see clearly for about ten inches without glasses.

Miss Liebowitz, now much better defined, turned out to be one of my first 'dates.' Teachers were housed in Bachelor Officer's Quarters and the enlisted troops were told that they were off limits. With a shortage of single young officers, this didn't leave much social life for the teachers. Miss Liebowitz would sometimes invite her students to dinner at the Officer's Club, usually boys, always in pairs and always with parents' permission. In today's world, she probably would be in jail for this but it was harmless and even forced us to learn some social graces. I even learned to look at her face. To my surprise, she turned out to be quite a nice and interesting person in spite of being a teacher. I don't know if it was deliberate on her part but many of her male students began to think of her as a really nice teacher and less – well, a little less - an object of teen lust.

The base was a small world in a harsh climate with no outside social life. Father was Commander of the largest unit on the base. He encouraged his married officers to invite the teachers to social events at their homes even if they did not have high school kids. I got used to my teachers coming for dinner or parties at our house.

Things evened out for me in the 10th grade. I was now old enough (13) to get into the Teen Club and tall enough that kids in school stopped seeing me as some oddity. I still did not like PE class but could at least compete with some equality. They began to forget or disregard my age and I began to be included in their activities. I guess because of the school surroundings I lost interest in kids my own age. For the first time since elementary school I enjoyed socializing with the group that I spent most of my time with. And vice versa.

The housing area on the base was dense with houses and I had a lot of friends nearby. I hated the weather and the dearth of activities but did enjoy a good circle of friends.

The base had a central steam plant that provided heat for everything. The houses all had old-fashioned radiators. Many of them had valves that no longer functioned – always stuck in the open position. It was weird to see the steam pouring out of opened windows when the temperature was 20 below but it was the only way to regulate the temperature at home. They ran all summer, too. I didn't mind this. At least at home I could get down to one layer of clothing and no shoes.

There was not a lot to do in Newfoundland. The year we arrived they had 33 feet of snow. It was usually bitterly cold and windy. I went to school in the dark and came home in the dark. Summers and school vacation time were better. Now it never got dark, most, but not all, of the snow melted and the temperature sometimes would soar into the 60s.

Father bought an old wooden boat and a 1933 Evinrude motor. This cast-iron behemoth was started with a rope. It had so much compression that it was designed to start on one cylinder, if you were lucky, and then switched to run on both. In the cold, it sometimes cooperated and sometimes not. It had no neutral – when it ran, you went. To stop you turned it off. Naturally, you couldn't start this thing tied to the dock. Sometimes we floated out to sea while Father sweated over this machine. I learned a few words that I never, ever heard him repeat again.

He and I would go fishing and ran a string of lobster traps just outside the base harbor. It is possible to get sick of lobster. We worked these traps as a team. We pulled them up and Father would reach in and grab the lobsters behind the head out of range of the claws. My job was to grab the claws and stick a wooden peg in the joint so they could not 'bite'. I needed one hand to hold the claw and one for the peg. You may have noticed that lobsters have two claws. We had endless debates over who had the crappier job. When I insisted we change jobs the damned things would 'bite' me before I could grab them. I stuck with getting one bite instead of two.

The bay froze for much of the winter. Father pulled the boat up to a protected storage area for the winter. When we went back the next summer, the boat was gone. Father was not pleased and sent the MPs out to find it. They soon located it in the garage of a sergeant. The poor man had bought a boat legitimately but hauled the wrong boat home. He had spent the entire winter refurbishing this boat until it looked like new. Father paid him for his time and materials. The sergeant had to find the boat he actually bought and start all over again.

Father also bought a small cabin from a local guy to use for moose hunting. The cabin was on the edge of 'town' and not of much use in that location. As part of a 'training mission' Father had a heavy lift helicopter pick up the cabin and move it to the center of a large island in the middle of a river about 20 miles from the base. I was in school and missed this but it apparently was quite a show for the people of Stephensville.

Father and I, usually with a few of his friends, would go out to this cabin during moose hunting season. Most of these friends went hunting but a few only wanted to stay in the cabin to ward off the cold with a 'wee nip'. I had no desire to be stumbling through the trees with a guy in the area who had a wee nip and a loaded gun, so this was fine with us.

Getting to the cabin required wading across about 50 yards of rushing water. This river was not too deep but moved swiftly and was very cold. The bottom seemed to be covered with slime covered bowling balls. On the inaugural visit to this cabin just Father, Mother and I went. Father got up early the next morning and shot a moose nearby. He cut it into large chunks and, mission accomplished, announced that it was time to go home. Mother didn't find this cabin all that comfortable anyway.

She crossed the river in a very large pair of borrowed rubber waders. Father stuffed large bloody hunks of moose into the back and front of her waders and told her to head for the car parked on the other side. It was quite a sight. The sound of the rushing water drowned out the language. It was Mother's only trip to the cabin.

While moose meat is OK, a moose seems to have an awful lot of it. Steaks, roasts, hamburger, sausage and moose loaf. Father's philosophy was that "if you kill it, you eat it." We ate it for a year. Just when we thought we had seen the last of it, Father shot another one. Mother announced that she was really glad that he had shot his LAST moose. Even he agreed after another year of moose meat – or so we thought.

Harmon AFB was a SAC (Strategic Air Command) base. Its main function was to provide a home for a fleet of B-52 bombers loaded with atomic bombs. At any time, a number of these planes flew over the north coast of Russia where they circled for hours ready to retaliate if the Cold War became a hot war. They would be refueled in mid-air and could stay in the air for as long as the crews could function. As they returned, other B-52s replaced them. With staggered schedules the runway was usually busy.

One weekend Father got a call at home. Somehow a moose had gotten through the fence surrounding the base and was wandering around the runway. What should they do? The thought of a tired B-52 crew plowing into a moose with a load of atomic bombs was not at all pleasant. Father left the house, ordered up a driver and jeep with a 50 cal. machine gun mounted on the rear and went moose hunting on the runway. He solved that problem with a single shot. However, you could not give moose meat away. Believe me, we tried. Another year of moose meat.

I also belonged to the Boy Scouts the first summer. The base was huge with large areas of unused forests. The Scouts had a camp made up of more or less permanent Army tents located deep in the woods next to a lake. I liked the Scouts because we were grouped by age and not grade. I had my one swimming experience in Newfoundland on a Scout camping trip. There was a boat on the lake for the Scouts. The leader took a group of us out to the lake center. The water was crystal clear and about 15 feet deep. It was a Newfoundland heat wave that day, maybe 65 degrees. Somebody decided that we should jump in. Nobody had a swimming suit. There was no pool on the base and this was in the middle of nowhere. We all took off our clothes and, on the count of three, jumped in. I thought my heart had stopped! Talk about cold! I got to the bottom, turned and kicked off. When I surfaced some of the boys were having difficulty getting back into the boat. I came out of the water like a dolphin at Sea World and practically landed on my feet in the boat. I don't think any boy was in the water more than 30 seconds. The Scoutmaster was on the verge of wetting his pants laughing. There was a mad scramble to get dressed and nobody was too picky about whose clothes they put on. Once back on shore I spent the afternoon shivering in a sleeping bag to get warm again. I loved swimming in Hawaii and Texas but the only water that touched me for the next three years came out hot from a shower head.

We discovered something else on those camping trips. Scattered throughout this remote area of the base were fenced enclosures about ten feet square. Inside was evidence of a deep hole filled with groundwater. The fences had metal signs attached with the symbol for radiation. It appeared to me that the U.S. government was disposing of nuclear waste by burying it in remote areas of this U.S. base in Canada. Harmon closed a few years later and was turned over to the Canadian government. I have never seen any mention of these sites and wonder if they were removed, abandoned or just hidden.

On a road trip back in the States with all of us Father bought a dachshund puppy. At the vet to get the required shots so that it could cross the border back into Canada, he discovers that the puppy is too young to get all of the needed shots. The vet was very helpful.

"Look, the puppy is perfectly healthy. Just stuff this pill down

the dog about 30 minutes from the border and it will sleep peacefully through the border crossing. You can get the shots later."

Father was one of the worst liars around but he saw that giving the puppy up would have put him in the doghouse. We headed back and, as ordered, stuffed this pill down the dog. In about 20 minutes it was in a deep sleep. We covered it with blanket and some other light stuff as we approached Canada's border station. Father pulled into the station, rolled down the window and said to the Immigration Officer, *"Hello. I don't have a dog."*

The Immigration Officer looked amused as he peered into the car at three kids and a wife. *"Don't believe I asked. Proceed."*

This dog, later named 'Junior', grew to be a fine pet. He tolerated being left alone for about an hour. Longer than that and he would grab the end of the toilet paper to run throughout the house with it, making an interesting mess. He also had a good nose. One evening Mother and Father went to a party down the street. It was close so they walked. Junior wanted out later that evening to pee, or so I thought. He never came back. A few minutes later I got a call from the Mother at the party. The dog had tracked them to the house and joined the fun. Eventually all the guests left for home except the unnoticed Junior. The hosts went to bed and during the night Junior joined them. We got a call in the morning to tell us not to worry about the missing dog. More interestingly, the hostess awoke to find Junior's nose almost in her ear. She laid there waiting for her husband to wake up, open his eyes and focus on Junior's little brown butt an inch from his nose.

When one of the neighbors bought the latest foreign car, a Volkswagen Beetle, my father got weary of listening to stories of its great gas mileage. He gave me a job. In the freezing night, I had to sneak out of the house and pour a gallon or two of gas into this Beetle. The neighbor bragged even more about the terrific mileage on his car. After a month or so of this my job changed. Now I had to sneak out and remove gas from the car. The bragging disappeared. Then a week before this neighbor's birthday, my father sent me out at night to steal the hubcaps from the car. The neighbor called the MPs and complained loudly about the theft. For his birthday, my father presented him with his hubcaps in a nicely wrapped box.

My junior year in High School was really a good one – for awhile. About halfway through the year Mother developed serious pain in one hip. She was only 34 years old. The base hospital did everything they could but couldn't diagnose the cause or find a cure. They sent her to Walter Reed in Washington, DC. Her two week trip turned into about 4 months. Sister Nina was in kindergarten but Lisa was still at home. At first neighbors helped out but as time went on Father had to find another solution. He hired a housekeeper but she went home as soon as I got back from school. We went to the

Officer's Club to eat but that soon exhausted both of us. My father could burn water on the stove so in self defense I began to learn to cook. Between cooking, babysitting and school I didn't have much time for myself.

When Mother did return, I realized how bad it was. She no longer could stand on that leg and any movement was very painful. My schedule didn't change because she really wasn't able to do much. She took a lot of painkillers and soon began to augment them with Jim Beam. I think my father was just lost in all of this. He asked for a transfer to an area with a good hospital.

Oklahoma

We arrived at Tinker AFB in Oklahoma City in the spring of 1961. Housing was not available on the base so we moved into a rented house on Ercoupe Drive in Midwest City. The house was only a few blocks from the main gate of the base. Mother was now in a wheelchair. I had a month or two left in my junior year. I enrolled in the local district Midwest City High School. To my surprise I needed only a few classes to graduate. The base school in Newfoundland had 8 classes a day while Oklahoma schools only had six. Therefore I had completed 4 years of Oklahoma high school in three. There was a requirement for 4 years of some subjects – English and history, if my memory is correct. The school even suggested that I could take these two courses in the summer and graduate. After all the years I dealt with the age thing in school, absolutely the last thing I wanted was to be a 15 year old college freshman! Fortunately my parents didn't think much of the idea either.

I discovered that this school was generally behind the one I came from. In most of my classes the new material was essentially a review of things I had already learned. It was a boring few months. It was a big school but, in spite of its location next to a large AFB, it had only a handful of military kids. The base sat in another school district so the kids on the base went there. I didn't have much in common with the kids in my classes. The major activity for high school boys here seemed to be to get a car or truck and drive around. For the girls, it seemed to be to ride around with the boys. It would be the last half of my senior year before I would be old enough to drive anything.

Still, I did develop a circle of good friends. Jerry Osborne lived a few blocks away and he didn't mind picking me up in his car. Jerry's father worked at a Ford dealer so Jerry always had a good car. I had the hots for his younger sister, Marjorie. He would pick up his date and the four of us would go to movies, drive-ins and the usual hangouts. I also liked a girl named Sandy but that was short lived. The first – and last – time I asked her out, I went to her house and met her father. He was some fundamentalist preacher who told me his daughter did not dance, drink, watch movies or stay out past 7 o'clock. Maybe she did when he wasn't looking but I never found out.

In October 1961 a house became available on the base. We moved but there was no school bus to my school since we were in a different district. I really didn't want to change schools yet again and this was my last year. Each morning Father drove me to school because I could not get a driver's license until December. I took the English and history that I needed but had a problem filling the day. I had already taken almost everything this school offered while in Newfoundland. I took an Advanced

Placement (AP) physics class, an AP biology class and volunteered to be a teacher's assistant in another biology class. That still left an empty hour but I refused to take something like a Shop class just to fill time. The school agreed and let me leave early. This meant Father could pick me up on his late lunch hour. This arrangement did have an advantage for me. Father was so sick of this schedule that on my 16th birthday he bought me a car, handed me the keys and said *"Here. Drive yourself!"*

Mother spent a lot of time at the base hospital. She and the doctors agreed that it was time to deal with the problem and forget the cause. Hip replacements were a new experimental surgery with mixed results. She was tired of the pain and the wheelchair. She decided to have the damaged parts of her hip removed and the femur and pelvis fused. The joint would not move, of course, but she would be able to stand, walk and be hopefully pain free. The surgery was not complicated but the recovery required that the fused parts be absolutely immobile until the bones fused. She ended up in a cast that went from her armpits to her toes and stayed in this cast for about 6 months. They weaned her off of the painkillers and the Jim Beam wasn't available in the hospital. Father and I took turns visiting with her because Nina and Lisa were not allowed. She was often discouraged – she still was only 37 – and frustrated and in pain. She wasn't easy to deal with. However at the end of the process she was pain free and able to walk.

I graduated from high school and spent the summer working as a Headstart teacher in a poor downtown neighborhood. Obviously Headstart was desperate. I hadn't decided what to study in college but left this job knowing that it would not be teaching five year olds.

When I look back now on my childhood from a perspective of 60+ years, I see that I was often a lonely child. The constant moving was interesting and forced me to develop social skills not usually found in children but it prevented those lifelong friendships that develop when surrounded throughout childhood by friends and relatives.

I started at the University of Oklahoma (OU) in September 1962. College turned out to be a real shock. Through high school, other than two times that an English teacher assigned a book that I could not finish reading in school, I never took my books out of the school or did homework at home. Missing a class would be reported to your parents.

OU was obligated under state law to take any Oklahoma student who graduated in the upper 50% of the class. This was not exactly a high standard. The University realized that many, if not most, of the entering freshman would never finish. They devised a triage system to attempt to weed out the students who probably would not finish all four years. It did work – only 25% of the freshmen returned for the second year. The school accomplished this weeding out by making the first year one of the most difficult. Freshman classes were of course very large, no attendance was taken and a lot of material came from the professor, not the books and the testing rigorous. A substantial number of these new freshmen knew within weeks that they were doomed, gave up studying and just partied until the ax fell. Of the approximately 6,000 people who entered OU with me, about 1,500 returned for a second year and only about 1,000 ultimately graduated.

I never developed self-discipline in public school because I could make good grades without much work or study. Suddenly I am 17, away from home and surrounded by some pro-class hell raisers. All students under the age of 21 (meaning for me my entire college career) were required to live on campus. By November the majority living in my dorm knew they were doomed and decided to make the most of the opportunity to live until the end of the semester without parents, jobs or responsibility. I came very close to joining their numbers and just squeaked through with the grade point average to stay on.

One of the other residents of my dorm had assembled a long list of Biblical references that he claimed all organized religions just ignored because they didn't suit their purposes. I don't know if it was true or not but he claimed to have been ejected from a church that declared 'every word of the Bible is true.' He said that he brought up a few of the things he found and was told to leave

I don't remember all of the things he found but I did look up a few of them. The story of Onan – misinterpreted often to terrify teenage boys – where God kills Onan for not impregnating his brother's wife. In another passage God enjoins his followers to each have a male and female slave – but only from another country. This apparently does not sit well with the Canadians. Going to hell for touching a pig's skin can ruin a good football game. It sealed my opinion of religion until I went to Asia.

The second semester was better. The dorm was clear of most, but not all, of those who would be dropouts. By the end of the first year I was doing much better but I also realized that next year the dorm would be once again filled with doomed freshmen and the cycle would start again. I knew that I had to get out of the dorms if I ever was to have peace and quiet to get serious about the work.

I shared my dorm room with Fred Johnson, a red-haired Okie from Muskogee. A great guy, Fred was a year ahead of me, a serious student and a stabilizing influence. He worked at a sorority dining room. When he was in the room I tended to settle down and study because that is what he did. Unfortunately his hours meant that I often had wandered off before he came back to the room.

During the summer I worked at a place that repaired washers and dryers (handy in the coming years). I also worked on

Father. I finally convinced him that, rules or not, I had to get out of the dorm. He wrote the required letter to the university claiming that I now lived at home and commuted.

Fred (already 21) and I, along with two others, rented an apartment near the university. Over the next three years the two of us continued the arrangement. I'm convinced that I never would have finished my degree living in the dorm. After the first year I worked at Sears in the evening, leaving little time for socializing.

For many people, university was a time of great fun and memories. For me, it is now all a blur of long boring hours studying, sitting in classes and prowling the library. There are a few incidents I treasure.

Fred fell in love with a Jewish girl and they became engaged. A day or so after the engagement Fred and I were reading when he suddenly asked me a question.

"Kass, before we get married they aren't going to ask me to..uh.. to get..uh..you know?"

Fred wasn't circumcised. I couldn't resist.

"Oh, absolutely!"

The next day Fred came through the door throwing books and canned goods at me. *"You SOB! I didn't sleep at all last night!"*

Fred reluctantly brought this exceeding tender subject up and got a second opinion from his fiancée that differed from mine. I didn't get it — she thought it was funny.

At least Fred had a social life. Mine — as usual — was usually curtailed by the age thing.

It was Friday night and Fred wanted to visit his fiancée. His car wasn't running so he asked to borrow mine. I had an Isetta convertible — a tiny, bubble-shaped two-passenger car with the door in the front. It was powered by a one cylinder motorcycle engine.

Fred stayed out late and I never heard him come in. In the morning I made coffee and sat looking out the window over the golf course. My car is sitting in the parking lot with all of the flags from the golf course sticking out of the top. Fred had detoured on the way home by driving all over the golf course collecting the flag at each hole.

At the end of four years I was short one major class to graduate. I'd enrolled in Spanish (two years of a foreign language was required for graduation), done poorly and dropped the course. My instructor told me that some people just don't have an aptitude for languages. I think this is more a comment on how they teach than on my aptitude, as events subsequently proved. In any case I'd completed three semesters of Spanish, doing poorly but adequately in them, and still needed that last semester. I admit I hated the class, taught by instructors that couldn't speak the language and seemed more concerned with verb endings than communication. In any case, I needed an extra semester to finish up.

I finished all requirements in December 1966. Graduation is held only once a year so my degree says '1967.' A snowy day that December changed the direction of the rest of my life.

I saw no reason to just have one class so I had enrolled in several that interested me. On this morning it snowed and was cold and windy. I had an hour between classes, just short enough to make the trip back to the apartment not worth the effort. I went to the Student Union to get warm and have coffee. The Student Union wasn't normally packed but the weather drove a lot of students there that day. I got coffee but couldn't find a place to sit down.

In the hall a young Black girl sat at a booth for the Peace Corps. We started to talk – I wasn't really very interested. She invited me to take a test for the Peace Corps. It took about 45 minutes and would give me a warm place to sit. With nothing better to do, I did just that. The test had two parts. The first seemed to be basic US history, the second some sort of silly word games. (This turned out to be a MLAT language aptitude test. I made a very high score on it. Take that, Spanish class!) I handed in the test, went off to my next class and promptly forgot about the whole thing.

The Vietnam War was heating up and the government had restarted the draft. While I was in college I had a deferment but this would end soon. In an effort to make the draft fairer and to allow people to better plan, a drawing of birthdates was held. In the drawing my birthdate came up as 315, virtually assuring me –then anyway- that I would not be called. My classification would remain 1A, the top classification, but so far down the list that I could plan on not being drafted.

Finished with school, with a degree in psychology with minors in zoology and chemistry, I packed up and went home. I decided that I needed a month to unwind before the job hunt began. At the end of January I received a letter from the Peace Corps inviting me to train for two years service in Sabah. I had two months to respond. I never heard of Sabah and could not find it in any atlas or reference book. Intrigued, it went to the library and still could find nothing. Finally I asked the librarian. She knew that 'Sabah' was the new name of British North Borneo, changed after one day of independence before joining the nation of Malaysia. It sounded really interesting but, like the Army, most likely a waste of two years' time.

When I began to job hunt, the draft turned out to be a huge problem. Every potential employer asked for my draft status. The minute they saw '1A' they lost all interest, assuming that hiring me presented too many problems. First, they thought it likely that I would be called to service and no explanation of the new birthdate system made any impression. Second, the law required that they hold the job for me if I was drafted, obligating them to re-employ me after military service. It only took a couple of job interviews for me to get the picture.

The Peace Corps was looking better each day. I still thought it would be interesting and the draft gave me a good excuse. I decided to accept the offer. As soon as I did, I became very enthusiastic about it.

Me and My Draft Board

Viet-Nam was heating up and the draft called thousands in each month. The Peace Corps did not provide a deferment from the draft. While I knew that I probably would not be drafted, the Peace Corps did not and insisted that each Volunteer have a deferment from the local Draft Board. Each of the thousands of draft boards around the country was free to provide or deny a deferment and the policies were uneven. I took my Peace Corps letter down to the draft board in Oklahoma City. Behind the desk stood a dried up old prune of a woman with a frown on her face. I explained the situation. *"Sorry,"* she said, *"No deferment."*

I knew that there was an appeal process. *"I want to make an appeal to the secretary of the draft board."*

"That's me. Denied."

"Then I have a right to ask to meet with the members of the draft board. Give me a date."

It was clear that she took this as a personal affront. She slammed a few papers around but did give me an appointment.

Six rather elderly men sat on the board. At the appointed time I met with them, explained that the Peace Corps only accepted about 3% of the applicants, it was still government service and that I thought it served the country as well as the military. They agreed. They ordered the secretary, who attended but did not participate, to give me a one year deferment. I would remain category 1-A but not be called.

This secretary of the draft board would prove to be an ongoing problem. Well in advance of the end of the one year deferment I had to repeat this entire process again by mail. The second time the board gave me a deferment to the last day of my Peace Corps service.

I had one last brush with the military before I left Oklahoma. The Peace Corps sent me a standard Army medical form and a letter directing the local Military Induction Center to process me through the medical exam. The form had a large red "PC" stamped on the front. I arrived at the center and handed my papers to the Army private sitting at the desk. He directed me down the hall to a large room. Large signs on the wall directed me and about 100 other young men to remove all our clothing except one piece of underwear, store the clothes in the lockers around the wall and get in line. I joined the line shivering – it was February – clutching my medical form. Another Army private walked down the line looking at each person's form.

When he examined my medical form, he said *"Follow me."*

He took me to the head of the line where they measured blood pressure. He continued to lead me through the entire process, going room to room. I thought this was really a nice gesture for the future Peace Corps Volunteer until I overheard him talking with one of the clerks along the way. The clerk asked, *"What the hell is 'PC'?"*

"I have no idea but I'm not taking any chances!" So much for professional courtesy. I saw no reason to explain it to him.

The last room was the one most famous in Induction Centers. There were tape marks on the floor and we were asked to stand on one of them. My 'friend' took me to the front row. There were three rows of men. A doctor entered and shouted, *"Turn around, drop your underwear, bend over and spread your cheeks!"* Turn around? The doctor took entirely too much time to leisurely walk the rows and inspect for hemorrhoids. I could have told him that the guy in front of me did not have any. I left with a paper that said I had ten fingers, ten toes, two testicles, a heart that beat, a mouth that opened and an ass that closed. Some physical.

When my departure day arrived, Mother and Father took me to the airport for the flight to Hilo, Hawaii. Not a bad place for training, I thought. As they called the flight, Mother turned to me and said, *"Don't go and marry something with a bone in her nose."* Father leaned over and very quietly said, *"I wish I could go with you."*

The Peace Corps

I loved the mornings. No tiptoeing twilight here. The morning arrives in a symphony of awakenings. The shadow of the night races down the sides of the Crocker Range, sweeping across the valley, small villages and padi fields. The mild solar heat creates breezes that set a million jungle trees moving with a rushing sound of waving leaves, the click and clack of bamboos. Roosters crow and water buffalo begin to stir. The arriving light streams through the glassless window and warms the face, turning pink the light behind closed eyelids. I stir, stiff from sleeping on the bamboo floor with only a sheet for cover. Rolling onto my side – a mistake since I haven't developed toughened skin over my hip bones – I can see across the shiny bamboo floor smoothed by bare feet. The smell of Stella's cooking fire arrives through the cracks in the bamboo walls between the kitchen and house.

From the bedroom he shares with his wife, Fred ambles out stretching and scratching himself. Dressed only in a brilliant multi-colored brief swimming suit that he uses for daily underwear, he is all fine bones, muscle and clear brown skin. He glances out the window, ruffles his hair and murmurs *"Good morning"* to me.

As I sit up on the floor, Stella emerges from the kitchen with a tray holding cold rice from the night before, a plate of fried eggs and fish and a pot of hot tea. Stella has a huge, wonderful smile. She is a softer, less angular version of Fred. She gives Fred and me a mildly disapproving look – I'm wearing no more than Fred – and disappears back into the kitchen for plates and cups. Fred and I slip on shorts and move to sit on a large woven fiber mat in the center of the room that serves as the dining table.

At first the lack of furniture was uncomfortable. Unused to sitting and sleeping on the floor, I envied the flexibility and ease that even heavily pregnant Stella showed. After the few months I'd been in Sabah, I have lost a lot of weight. With no scales I don't know what I weigh now but all of the clothes I brought are useless. I wear the same kind of clothes bought at the market that everybody else has. The stretching needed to sit on the floor has finally eased the discomfort of doing so.

In the corner of the room, a pile of sheets and blankets begins to move. Geoffrey, the son of a neighbor, emerges. I had forgotten that he came to visit last night and fallen asleep. I still found it strange that children wandered about freely, eating and sleeping where they wished, while parents did not worry. Geoffrey is dressed in ragged shorts too big and a long ago white shirt too small, held shut by the single remaining button. He joins us, sitting by my side. The four of us begin to eat, still in the fog of the morning awakening.

Fred and I begin to discuss the plans for the day. Today we would add partitions to the house for a second bedroom for me. Geoffrey's small hand slides over to my arm, where he gently tugs at the downy hair. Geoffrey was about 9 or 10 years old. Every kid in Tambunan did this if they were close. It provides endless amusement. The Kadazan population is universally hairless on arms, legs and chest. Geoffrey meant no harm in satisfying his curiosity but this action always made me feel like some big, hairy pet ape. I just put up with it.Fred and I, along with a stream of neighbors and friends, had built this

 simple house. It stood on posts about four feet above the ground, with bamboo floors and walls. We moved in with a borrowed roof of tin that Fred needed to return.

Stella and the women neighbors would weave the palm fronds for the roof to replace the tin. Altogether the house had a few hinges and nails, otherwise everything came from the surrounding forests. It is comfortable and simple. We moved in with only the one large room and kitchen. The kitchen sat on the ground, reached by a short ladder in the house. The stove, just a platform made of mud and grass, held the fire. Fred had constructed a few shelves for a pantry. The only cost of construction was food to feed the people who showed up to help.

A lot had happened in the last five months.

Peace Corps training in Hawaii had been both physically and mentally exhausting. We began at 7 in the morning and it often ran until late at night. Our small group was split into two sections. Medical technicians and nurses make up one group, agriculturists the other. You could stick what I knew about agriculture in your eye without a tear but there I was. For three months we labored away at Malay language, tropical agriculture, ethnic sensitivity and culture. It was a non-competitive atmosphere where we all wanted each person to succeed. The staff of former Peace Corps Volunteers from Africa and South America (?) and imported Malay language teachers worked to see that each person absorbed as much as possible. In the end only one person was 'deselected.' John was a graduate of Cornell University's Tropical Agriculture School, the only person in the ag group with even a hint of actual qualifications. John, however, had a Beatle haircut and made it clear that his hair was a non-negotiable issue. Ah, the uptight segment of the 60s.

There were a lot of touchy-feely mind games. We each spent a night in an isolated hut to 'think over our commitment.' Exhausted, I took the opportunity to get some good sleep. We were asked to rank each other and, as a group, refused to do it.

We plowed the ground behind a water buffalo, built outhouses, paddled canoes, cared for chickens, hiked the Hawaiian jungle, showered in ice cold water, were punctured weekly for every disease that had a shot, ate Army food to fatten us up, built a local Community Center, practiced teaching farming at local schools, visited pig farms, gave each other haircuts and did it all for $12.50 a week. Only Sundays were free. Most of us ended up at the local Hilo Planter's Bar, the only place in Hilo that would cash our checks. They usually ended up keeping most of the money.

This three month marathon forged friendships that have survived 40 years now. Tired and cranky, at the end we were sworn into the Peace Corps by a local judge, piled onto an airplane to Honolulu for three days at a pre-paid hotel and given, yes, $12.50. We were allowed to ship 100 lbs. by air freight to Sabah but most of us had no money to buy anything to ship. On the flight to Hawaii, the Peace Corps forgot to allow us to bring 100 extra pounds. The Peace Corps supplied a large trunk. I had a few extra clothes and a typewriter that I placed into the trunk with a lot of wadded up newspaper.

We flew to Japan, changed planes and spent the night in Hong Kong. Mostly broke, we wandered the streets of Kowloon and admired the displays of Rolex and Nikons. The next day we boarded a Malaysian-Singapore Airlines flight to Kuala Lumpur. The airline flew British Comets, the first commercial jet, notable for shedding its wings mid-flight. Before boarding they carefully weighed each of us, just to add to our confidence. At the 4 foot high narrow door a stewardess held a pillow at the top for those who did not listen to her admonishment to duck down. We were ordered to arrive in coats and ties. When the door of the aircraft opened in Kuala Lumpur the rush of humid hot air, combined with a few free drinks along the way, just about caused a general collapse. We boarded a bus and were driven to the Country Peace Corps Director's house for a welcoming cocktail party. In the heat, tired from a 36 hour trip, most of us fell asleep.

The next morning we said goodbye to those volunteers assigned to work in the Malaysian peninsula. We boarded a fleet of small taxis bound for Malacca. The roads were excellent but narrow. This could have been a great way to see the countryside but at 85 mph I was too terrified to see much. Malacca was interesting and historic and small enough to see on foot in an afternoon walk. It is full of historic post-colonial Portuguese government buildings painted in a macho pink.

History lesson

The Portuguese were the first colonists, founding Malacca and Macau in the 1500s. They seemed to have a knack for getting it wrong. They established themselves in Malacca to use the river as a port. In a very few years silt filled the river to the point that their ships could no longer enter. A short distance away is

Singapore, one of the world's great natural ports. The British got there first.

Macau is located on the Pearl River and was established as a base for trade with Imperial China and Japan. River silt fills its harbor and requires constant dredging to be useful. A few miles away, across the mouth of the same river, is Hong Kong and its superb harbor and, again, the British got there first – only 200 years after the founding of Macau. For a few years Portugal was the world's first and greatest colonial power in Asia and Africa but they were soon eclipsed by other European nations because of their poor choices of location. For example, England took India; Portugal took the tiny island of Goa! (end)

Rested, we reluctantly climbed into another fleet of taxis to continue on to Singapore. These taxis were in much poorer shape but unfortunately went just as fast. We arrived late in the day at the Singapore YMCA, spent the night and departed early the next day by air for Jesselton, the capital o f Sabah.

We had a few days to explore the area, try out our Malay language, rest and meet the Peace Corps staff. When discussing possible assignments, I asked for the most remote place possible, thinking that I might as well do the Peace Corps experience to the maximum.

The nurses split off to go their own ways. My group was now down to about 8 people. The Department of Agriculture arranged a three week 'orientation' at various places along the coast. Impressed by this welcome, it took awhile to learn that they actually hadn't made any arrangements for our postings and needed time to get ready. We were accompanied by local Agriculture Specialists who would be paired up with us for assignment. None of us knew with whom we would eventually work. After ten days the Agricultural Specialists returned to Jesselton for their assignments without knowing with which Peace Corps Volunteer they would live with for the next two years.

After being shuttled around the coast with nothing really to do we received our assignments. Tambunan was the most remote place they had. It turned out not to be remote in the classic sense, just damned hard to get to! I first took the steam train to Penampong. Built by the British around the end of the 19th century, the engine had recently been renovated. It was beautiful to look at but moved slowly and belched cinders that burned holes in clothing. It rattled along the coast and then turned inland to follow the banks of a turbulent river. The slow pace gave me a chance to observe the fishing boats along the coast, rice padis and neat little villages. Midway, the train stopped for water. When I saw many of the passengers climb out for a track-side pee and smoke, I followed. As I stood by the thick jungle that came almost to the tracks, I heard a rustling. Out stepped two Murut young men dressed in nothing but a thin strip of red cloth around their hips and a few feathers in their hair. Each carried a blowpipe and a machete. They motioned for me to give them a cigarette. As I gave it to each one I thought to myself, *'What in the hell have you gotten yourself into!'* They smiled and disappeared into the trees. (For the record, over the next two years I never saw another Murut 'in the wild.')

I arrived in Penampong late in the day to be met by Father Michael Henslemanns. Father Henslemanns (known as 'Hensy' when he wasn't around) was building the first interior secondary school in the country in Tambunan. He drove, somewhat erratically, a Land Rover that carried us to Keningau, a drive of several hours. There was a light rain. The Land Rover had electric wipers with a manual handle in case they didn't work. They didn't. Hensy hunched over the steering wheel and periodically worked the nonfunctioning wiper blade with one hand. With almost no traffic on the road he tended to wander as he worked the wiper blade. I jokingly asked him which side of the road he drove on. *"The best side, of course,"* he responded.

We arrived in Keningau late in the day, ate together at a small restaurant and took an after dinner walk. Along the way, we passed a man who said to Hensy, *"Good evening, Father."* Turning to me he again said, *"Good evening, Father."* Hensy's reply was *"Look, man, he isn't a priest!"* I spent the night at the Government Guest House. Hensy stayed elsewhere but picked me up the next morning. The road from Keningau to Tambunan rapidly turned into a narrow dirt track that wound up and down hills. Leaves lashed at the sides of the Rover. We crossed

 several rivers with water squirting up through holes in the vehicle floor. We bounced through the jungle for about 4 hours before arriving in Tambunan. Well, almost arriving. Hensy dropped me off at the Agricultural Station, virtually the first place in the Tambunan Valley. This made it appear to me to be totally isolated.

Carrying my oddly out of place suitcase down the path to the station, I saw a man leading a buffalo. Before I could say anything, he tied the buffalo to a tree, reversed directions and ran back down the path. Soon Fred came ambling up the path to meet me. I met Fred during the orientation but this was the first time that either of us knew we would be paired together. We greeted each other and Fred grabbed my suitcase. He looked grim and unhappy. (He was hoping for somebody else?)

The station had several large classrooms, an office, a series of storage rooms, an acre of coffee seedlings and several acres of older rubber trees. We walked down a small embankment to the river plain to a small blue house that he and his hugely pregnant wife and I would share. Six or seven of the workers were eating lunch on the porch. Fred and the workers had been expecting me – well, expecting somebody – and instantly decided to take the rest of the day for an extended welcoming meal. Fred's wife, Stella, joined us. Fred and Stella spoke good English but the staff did not. I soon realized that Malay was their second language also. (Nothing like killing yourself to learn the wrong language!) Tambunan's people were Kadazan, the most numerous group in Sabah. I would soon learn that Kadazan is a much more difficult language, capable of nuances that Malay could not convey.

Around 4 o'clock the staff left. Fred, Stella and I continued sitting on the porch, getting to know each other. By 6 o'clock the sun started to disappear. So did Fred and Stella. They excused themselves, went into their room, closed the door and then the windows in spite of the warm evening. Feeling abandoned, I went into the other room, opened my suitcase to pull out a book and lit the kerosene lamp. Within moments I was covered with bugs attracted to the light. Closing the windows did little good since the walls did not quite reach the ceiling. By moving the lamp away I could read with fewer bugs on me. A few hours later, mostly from boredom, I blew out the lamp, brushed off as many of the bugs from the iron bed as I could see, laid down with just a sheet over me and drifted off to sleep.

 Morning came with a crash as the light suddenly appeared through the window. I woke up and dressed. On the porch Stella had already laid out breakfast. Fred didn't mince any words.

"Kass, this is a very bad place."

"Why?"

"There are dead people all around this house."

"Uh, what?"

Fred explained that the house and surrounding rubber trees were built in the middle of a Kadazan grave yard. Fred and Stella were uncomfortable during the day and terrified at night.

After breakfast, Fred took me on a tour. Throughout the rubber trees and around the house were large jars buried in the ground with the tops exposed. My interest in them did not impress Fred at all. There were dozens of them, one only a few feet from my bedroom. The tops were long broken and I saw nothing inside of them. According to Fred the Ag Station was a failure for many reasons but this was the primary one. It was difficult to employ workers. Those who did work refused to work on the rubber trees in the grave site. The house had been empty for several years because every Ag Dept. person assigned there refused to live in it. Fred had been given a choice – live in the house with the Peace Crops Volunteer or be fired.

Although Fred focused on the grave yard, the Ag Station was a failure for several other reasons. It was located much too far from the nearest villages. Its few workers arrived late and left early. By Ag Dept. decree it was to encourage rubber and coffee cultivation. Neither would be profitable in Tambunan because of transportation costs. Later I would learn that few people in Tambunan were interested in any cash crops. The station had classrooms to teach but no facilities for people to stay or cook. Again distance prevented any interest in ag courses. The entire operation was ill-conceived.

Fred, Stella and I lived there for about six weeks. I adapted to bathing in the river and using the outhouse. Fred and I had endless evening conversations about the 'huntus' or ghosts that he just knew wandered about after dark. I would go for a walk with a flashlight, partly out of boredom and partly to demonstrate that I could come back alive. Fred bought none of it, coming to the conclusion that Kadazan ghosts only bothered Kadazans. Fred and Stella continued to barricade themselves in their room at dusk. I was always welcome to visit after dark but they made it clear that I would not stand in the door to say good night. Open, out and slam!

I rapidly had my own serious misgivings. My request for a remote area wasn't meant to mean devoid of more than a handful of people. The Ag Station did almost nothing. It was a six mile walk to town to check my mail (and six miles back!) and took an entire day. With little to do and missing out on the experience of meeting an interesting and friendly population, I came close to either going home or asking for a transfer. Fred and I did two things simultaneously. He asked for permission to move into a village, using me as the excuse. 'My Peace Corps Volunteer doesn't like living here.' I wrote a hopefully convincing letter to the Peace Corps Director. I described the conditions at the Ag Station but said that I thought there was a great deal of work to be done in Tambunan. This was pure speculation on my part since I had been almost nowhere and seen little. In addition, in a 'nothing ventured, nothing gained' attempt I asked for transportation. Peace Corps had a worldwide policy of denying motorized transportation to Volunteers after a series of deaths in various countries by vehicle accident.

Peace Corps sent me a bicycle. This was an improvement but my next letter pointed out that Tambunan was a mostly narrow valley about ten miles long with no paved roads. Even with a bicycle I had never been beyond the town at midpoint. To my surprise the Peace Corps Director allowed the Dept. of Agriculture to issue me a motorcycle. All I had to do was come to Jesselton to collect it.

I decided to walk to Jesselton. At that time it was a two day trip so I joined a group of others and headed into the jungle. It was a friendly group of young people. Within an hour I felt like an elephant in a herd of gazelle. Effortlessly they walked along talking and looking around; occasionally a hand went into the heavy growth and reappeared with a fruit to eat. I crashed through the leaves unable to take my eyes off my feet, still tripping over roots and rocks. As we climbed higher, they broke out second shirts or jackets while I just dripped sweat.

In the late afternoon we reached a simple lean-to. My fellow travelers looked refreshed and cool. I was tired, sweaty and hungry. The others all wore flip-flops, the almost universal footwear. I had worn shoes for the climb. I took them off to expose scarlet socks. When I pealed these off, I had 5 or 6 land leaches on each foot. I was horrified but my companions didn't find this any big deal. I went to pull them off but was told to not do this. Somebody showed me that a glowing cigarette placed near the leach caused them to let go without further damage. Leaches have a chemical in their mouths that deadens feeling and prevents coagulation of the blood. I never felt them bite and the wounds bled copiously after they let go. I splashed everything with some borrowed Detol, an English version of Listerine. It took a long time for the bleeding to stop. Everybody brought out their food for the evening cold meal and shared. I had a large tin of sardines – a big hit.

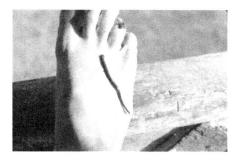

When darkness came we all bedded down for the night on the open platform of the lean-to, covered with sheets and towels. I didn't sleep much, bothered by the millions of mosquitoes and the sounds of God-knows-what moving through the jungle. Sabah has an abundance of wild life. I spent a lot of time in the jungle over the next two years and never saw a single animal in the triple canopy growth. I heard monkeys howl and birds chatter, always unseen.

In the morning I switched to the pair of flip-flops that I brought for use in the big city and left my shoes on the lean-to platform. Perhaps somebody got use from them – they were the last shoes I would wear before I left Sabah. The flip-flops were far more practical because I could see the leeches. There were millions of land leaches - I swear they can jump – but my ever-present cigarette usually got them before they got me.

Eventually we reached a dirt road under construction. The road would not reach Tambunan until months after I left the Peace Crops. Everybody stood around talking and waiting. As usual the others looked cool while I dripped in sweat. I sat down in the shade of the tall trees and removed my shirt to cool down. Within moments, dozens of beautiful large black butterflies appeared and landed all over my exposed body and face. Their long proboscis gently stabbed at my skin ineffectively. They seemed to think that I was some huge flower. I held still to watch their gently tickling efforts. It was a magical few moments.

On cue, a large empty Land Rover arrived to carry us down to Jesselton. I checked in at the Peace Corps office. They directed me to the Dept. of Agriculture office. A clerk handed me a document and directed me to a local motorcycle dealer. It was late in the afternoon before I found the place. I handed over the paper and they rolled out a brand-new Honda motorcycle. I was handed the keys and an Owner's Manual. Before I could say a word, the shop closed and the staff left.

I'd never ridden a motorcycle. I'd never even been a passenger on a motorcycle. With no idea how to operate this thing, I sat on the curb and went through the manual. It didn't look that difficult. Unlike a car, the gears shifted by foot and the clutch worked by hand. The front brakes worked by the other hand and rear by the other foot. Well, I had to do something; I couldn't sit here all night. I started it up, lifted the kickstand, put it into gear and gently let out the clutch. There wasn't much traffic as I headed off to Patt Brett's house. Shifting gears wasn't difficult but knowing when to shift gears was a little trickier. I jerked my way up to about 30 mph. At the first stop I applied the rear brakes and, in a panic, discovered they didn't do much. At the next stop I used the front brakes and nearly went over the handlebars. I got to Patt Brett's house in one piece.

Patt was a member of our group and ended up as the most misused Volunteer in Sabah. She was a skilled and experienced secretary. Instead of an assignment like the rest of us, she became the secretary for the Peace Corps Director. It gave her a nice two bedroom house but gave her little chance or time to met and interact with the local people. In my view, she ended up as cheap labor and missed most of the experiences that lead her to join the Peace Corps. She compensated by running her second bedroom as a Peace Corps hotel and listening to the often tall tales of visiting Volunteers.

I had a day to practice on the motorcycle before the train left for Penampang. I felt reasonably confident by the time the motorcycle was loaded on the train for the journey back to Tambunan. In Penampang I wasn't so confident as I thought over the drive ahead so I stayed there for the night. The road

from Penampang to Keningau is paved but lightly traveled. I headed out worried about breakdowns in the middle of nowhere. It is an entirely different experience between the enclosed Land Rover and a motorcycle. In the wide open air I began to think of snakes, elephants, rhinos and other real and imagined hazards of Sabah. The lack of traffic was not encouraging now. After I passed Keningau, these thoughts only enlarged as I hit the narrow winding dirt road. This, at least, made me proficient in gear shifting. Then I came to the first river. It was about 50 feet wide and a foot deep. The road crews had made a smooth stone crossing now slick with moss and rushing water. I thought of pushing the motorcycle across but realized that the water would go up the exhaust pipes and perhaps ruin the engine. I decided to ride across. As long as the water did not reach the air intake, the running engine should keep the water out of the exhaust. I was scared that the engine might stop midstream. With my feet down and the clutch slipping I entered the water. I made it! Cool!

I repeated this several more times and felt quite proud of myself as I pulled into the Ag Station.

Fred had been busy while I was gone. He had permission for us to move into a village. He had already made arrangements with the village chief to allow him to build a house about a mile east of the town. His outlook was much better now and the two of them were happy and relieved to not stay in the middle of the grave yard. I looked forward to living near town and other people. All we needed now was a house.

Dozens of people showed up. Working together, they dug holes for the support posts and drug in stacks of green bamboo. Working without nails, they cut cross beams to fit and lashed them into place with rattan strips. By the end of the first day the framework of the house was complete. Fred, Stella and I had purchased a big supply of rice, vegetables and chickens. Stella cooked and fed everybody.

The floor and walls were made of flattened bamboo. A slit is made up one side of the bamboo stalk and then it is flattened by whacking it with a parang (machete). The resulting panel is

free, durable and smooth. The added advantage to this type of floor is that dust and dirt fall through to the ground. It only took 3 or 4 days to build the entire house. With its borrowed roof we planned to move in the next day. Stella, however, had one more thing to do at the Ag Station.

We had come back from the new house and went down to the river to bathe. It was a nice day — well, OK, they all were nice days — and we lingered on the riverbank to air dry. Fred and I were in our usual swimsuit/underwear and Stella was wrapped in a big sarong. Suddenly Stella announced that the baby was coming. Predictably Fred looked unconcerned and I panicked.

"We have to get her to the hospital!"

"Why? She isn't sick. And there is no hospital."

Ooops. I hadn't thought of that.

Stella said, *"There is lots of time and the midwife is in the village up the road. Fred will get her."*

We helped Stella up the riverbank and back to the house. She lay down on the floor and Fred sort of ambled off in the direction of the village. *"Stella, don't you do anything until the midwife is here!"* Stella just smiled and then grimaced. I thought to myself, *'Oh, God, please no, not while Fred is gone.'* Well, Fred was gone for about two weeks, or so it seemed. He returned just before dark — alone.

The midwife was nowhere to be found. I suggested that Fred

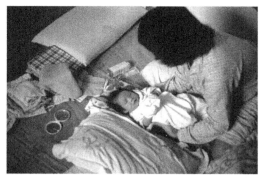

try harder to find her. With that, the shadow of the descending sun crossed the house to leave us in near darkness. Fred made it absolutely clear that he had made his last trip outside until daylight. (Those damned graves again!) Neither he nor Stella appeared concerned about the missing midwife. Fred suggested I go look for the midwife if I was worried. Of course I did not know who to look for or where to look.

I spent the night with Stella as she periodically groaned and moaned. Fred, incredibly, went to sleep. At about 3 in the morning, Stella's moans were coming much more frequently. Finally she slapped Fred awake and said that the baby was just about 'here.' Fred politely told me it was time to 'go away' so I left for my room.

For the next half hour or so I could hear Stella's muffled cries. Finally they stopped. In a few moments I heard a baby cry.

"It's a boy!" yelled Fred.
"Can I come and see?"
"Not yet. Wait awhile."

Finally Fred called me to come over. When I entered the room Stella and the baby were laying asleep on a clean mat. The other mat was covered with blood, afterbirth, soiled rags and other things I had no interest in. Forget that 'new baby' smell. There has to be a better way. Fred unwrapped his new son to show me all his parts. He was red and wrinkled with a flat nose and elongated head. I didn't think this baby was the least bit cute but cooed appropriately. Fred assured me that Stella and the baby were just fine so I went back to my room and collapsed.

We moved to the new house a few days later. The baby developed a nose and nice clear skin. There are no diapers here and, surprise, no diaper rash either. His solid messes were disposed of quickly. He did have a talent for shooting arcs of pee in unexpected directions at unexpected moments but the bamboo floor took care of that – unless, of course, you got targeted. It never bothered Fred or Stella to get hit and, after awhile, I also thought, *'Well, it's just pee,'* and it stopped bothering me, well, most of the time.

Things were going well. I had a lot of friendly neighbors, transportation to get around and, well, not much to do.

The People of Tambunan

Even after 40 years I find it difficult to describe the people of Tambunan without sounding idealistic and smitten with the culture which, of course, I was. The Kadazans were in a period of enormous change, some of it good and some of it not. I was there to see some of the old ways still followed. How I wish I had been there 50 years earlier! It seems that most of the old ways are now gone but at least I saw some during this time.

Most people lived in bamboo houses elevated on ironwood logs, although a few houses of planks were appearing. Traditional clothing had disappeared to be replaced with manufactured shorts or pants and shirts. Nobody could recall what they wore before the arrival of factory woven cloth. In the hundreds of photos I took while there, about half the people are barefooted, the rest with flip-flops and a very few with shoes. As I had already discovered, shoes had no advantages.

The villages had no electricity, plumbing or paved roads. Obviously there was no television, few radios (batteries were expensive) or newspapers. The mail was fairly reliable but Time and Newsweek were banned by the central Islamic government. Until Hensey opened the secondary school, there had been only two elementary schools that stopped at grade six. Perhaps 20% of the children attended them and few finished.

There was no doctor, one clinic staffed by a 'dresser,' a person with a bit of medical training and a supply cabinet of medicine that would fit into a briefcase. If emergency medical help was needed, the patient faced the 4 hour bouncing ride in a Land Rover through the jungle. There was one trip each day. My greatest fear was not disease (likely) but broken bones (also likely). The infant mortality rate was very high but dropping rapidly which caused other problems. I later lived with another family. The father told me his parents had 13 children and 3 survived to adulthood. He had 11 children and it looked as if they might all survive. Clearly Darwin's Theory worked here; if the children survived to age 5 or 6 they tended to become tough, hardy, disease resistant and strong. Still it was sad to see so many children die of diseases that were easily preventable or treated.

And there were children everywhere! Boys (but rarely girls) wandered around in groups and, like Geoffrey, might not go home for days. They were looked after by the whole village, eating and sleeping wherever they happened to be at nightfall. They were, without exception, well behaved, polite and helpful. They responded to any request from an adult cheerfully and without complaint. For example, when asked, Geoffrey hauled water, washed dishes, collected firewood and watched the baby. I don't think it ever occurred to him to not do it. On the other hand, I don't think it ever occurred to Fred or Stella to send him home or not offer him food or a place to sleep. I never saw children, or adults for that matter, fighting or squabbling. Human nature tells you that they must have had some disagreements but they must have been short and quickly forgotten.

Adults always reacted to me in an open and welcoming manner. Unfortunately the British left their mark. The older generation well remembered the recently departed British. Many would meet me, remove their hats and look at the ground when they spoke. The answer to anything was *"Yes, Tuan"* because I was White. (Tuan is a title of respect.) The younger adults were much easier to get to know but they also were convinced that I knew everything about every subject because I was White. Almost everybody thought all Whites were British, knowing little of any other country. The younger generation, including teenagers, was the easiest. Many people of all ages became friends, although I suspect few of them knew that I was barely out my teens. I sometimes asked people how old they thought I was. Inevitably they guessed in the 40s – I was 21! To me the saddest thing of all was the feeling of inferiority that I could clearly see in all but the young children.

If they only knew how much of the rest of the world wanted a society with many of their attributes! I didn't have much but I had many things that others did not – a camera, a small tape recorder, money (with little employment trading things was common). I always lived with a family and the house had people wandering in and out all day. With little furniture and no locks on anything I had to leave things out in the open. But not once in two years was a single thing ever missing. People were generous with what they had and not envious of what they didn't.

The morning after Stella gave birth, she asked Fred and I to continue working on the new house. We did so, returning at lunch to find that Stella had cooked and resumed her routine. So much for the trauma of birth!

We moved before the house was completed. Fred and Stella really wanted out of the graveyard. It only took a few trips to move clothes and cooking utensils. The furniture in the old house belonged there so we really didn't have much to move.

On the first night, Fred and Stella retired to their bedroom and I slept in the middle of the other room. Sometime in the night, I awoke to the gentle swaying of the house. There was no wind. Fred appeared in his usual brilliant underwear, mumbling and scratching in the light of his flashlight. He disappeared down the log we used for stairs. A few shouts under the house and the swaying stopped. Fred reappeared. *"Buffalo scratching themselves on the posts,"* he grumbled and went back to bed. We had the bamboo to build a fence around the house but had only completed about half of it.

In this country, we build fences to keep the animals in; in Sabah the fences are to keep the animals out. It is a sensible system that allows the wandering buffalo to keep the grass of the villages looking like golf courses. Barred from under the houses, the ever-present plops of buffalo poop stay nicely out of range.

We finished the fence, minus a gate, the next day with the help of the neighbors. The late afternoon habit became a leisurely half mile walk down to the river to bathe and change clothes, followed by the evening meal. My neighbors were all neat and clean at the end of the day, although clothing was often sun-faded and tattered. Lighter colored clothes sometimes looked dirty but were not. Everything was washed in the river but some stains did not come out.

This time I awoke during the night by a gentle rhythmic bouncing of the bamboo floor. Still half asleep, I heard a quiet long grunt from Fred and the bouncing stopped.

I've heard it said that you can get used to anything. That's just plain wrong. Fred and Stella's lovemaking could not have been helped by their knowledge that I was a few feet away on the resilient floor. Imagination is often better than reality. I got little sleep for the next few weeks. I'm sure they waited until they thought I was asleep while I couldn't sleep until they finished. This went on until we finished the construction of the second bedroom in the opposite corner of the house and I installed an iron bed that did not pick up the motion.

Up to this point I thought that Fred was a difficult and demanding husband. He expected Stella to cook, wash and take care of the house while, at home, he did little more than sit and wait for her to serve meals. Then Stella taught me how things really worked.

I came home one day to find Fred backed up against the wall while Stella wagged her finger under his nose and clearly was giving him hell. She chewed on him; he looked very uncomfortable and, to my surprise, took it while looking like a little boy getting scolded. When Stella did stop, Fred fled out the door. Stella stomped off to the kitchen. I looked through

the window to see Fred chopping on a pile of bamboo. Fred had never finished the gate to the fence around the house, the buffalo got inside and pooped all around under the house. Stella had her jobs and Fred had the right to complain if she didn't do them. Fred's job included finishing the fence and Stella had the right to give him hell if he didn't do his jobs. He took his scolding and never said a word back.

This was not to be the end of Fred's scolding. He was unable to finish a proper gate before nightfall so he used my bicycle to block the entrance. We had not yet gone to bed when we heard a great crashing and thrashing just outside the house. A young buffalo stuck his head through the frame of the bicycle to get at the longer grass growing inside the fence. His horns passed through but became entangled. Panicked by the thing now completely around his neck, he managed to push one foot through the front wheel and one foot through the back wheel. The buffalo is completely trapped, thrashing about and thoroughly trashing the bicycle. Fred took a look and headed for the neighbors for help. I took a look and headed for my camera. ('Who would ever believe this?')

It took 5 or 6 men to extricate the buffalo, leaving the bicycle a complete loss. The spokes of both wheels were broken or bent, the rims warped and the chain broken. That night, as I drifted off to sleep, I could hear Stella still giving Fred hell.

For a month or so, Fred and I commuted back and forth to the Ag Station but there really was little for either of us to do there. I began to spend more of my time in the town and the small Dept. of Agriculture Office there. The staff consisted of Paul and a few workers. He was very friendly, liked my company and moved about the valley offering assistance to the farmers. It was much more of the type of thing I had expected.

Fred decided to resign from the Ag Dept. after being offered a job as a 4th grade teacher at the school nearby. I had a visit from the District Agricultural Officer who was convinced that I had something to do with Fred's resignation. I did not. Fred, Stella, baby and I moved into a small plank house next to the school. This apparently was a perk for the teachers. Geoffrey moved with us. We were quickly joined by Ambrose, another boy about ten years old, who came from Monsok, a village a day's walk into the jungle. His parents wanted him to go to school but the boy had no place to stay.

Ambrose would walk back to Monsok on the weekends. He offered to take me with him – a chance to see a really remote place compared to Tambunan. We walked for about five hours through the jungle along a river, stayed the night and returned the next day.

On the third weekend, Ambrose (picture) returned home alone but did not come back to Tambunan. We later learned that he contracted some unknown disease and died within a day.

Fred taught for only two months. Stella was not happy in Tambunan. She wanted to return to Jesselton. Fred resigned again, packed up and they left. The three of us had gotten along well but I always felt that there was some small barrier.

I needed another place to live. I could not stay in the teacher's house and the place we built had been given to another family. I looked around but felt uncomfortable with the idea of just asking somebody if I could live with them. Paul, from the Ag Dept. office, lived with some of his relatives and I thought they probably didn't need yet another person.

I got my mail from Sarus, the District clerk. He handled the mail, paperwork for land titles and a dozen other functions.

While collecting my mail I discussed the housing problems with him – he knew everybody. He told me that he had two houses. One was near the town where he stayed with some of his 11 children during the week and the other was located on some rice padi land he owned and where his wife stayed. He invited me to stay in the town house for a few dollars rent each month. It sounded like an ideal arrangement.

Sarus had 8 daughters and 3 sons. The two older boys lived in the town house more or less permanently and went to school. The older daughters sort of rotated between houses, sharing the cooking, cleaning and other household duties. They did not go to school. I never knew who or how many people would be in the house when I returned in the evening. It took me a time to figure out who his children were, given the constant influx of friends and other children who dropped in for days at a time. I used to joke that I lived there for a month before Sarus noticed. Not true but possible.

Sarus spoke fine English. His oldest son, Zainol, was about 12 years old. Zainol's English was poor and it soon became clear that part of my 'rent' was to improve this. He had a quick mind and eagerness to learn and soon became quite fluent. The Peace Corps supplied me with a box of about 75 paperback books. Zainol methodically

went through them, driving me crazy in the evenings with his constant *"What does this word mean?"* The Peace Corps never thought to include a dictionary in the box. Sometimes I would drift off to sleep on the floor with Zainol sitting next to my head reading by the light of a tiny kerosene lamp, stopping occasionally to poke the book into my face with his finger on some word he didn't understand.

In self defense I asked Sarus to construct a small room in the corner of the house for me to sleep. The Peace Corps finally provided some money for furniture so that I had a bed, a desk and a small table with four chairs that stayed in the center of the house. When I retreated into this room to sleep, Zainol and the other kids would leave me in peace – usually. Sleeping required a routine. I usually read for awhile so I would climb into bed with a small kerosene lamp. The mosquitoes were awful so I would carefully tuck the bottom of the mosquito net under the mattress. I would read for awhile and then blow out the lamp. Without fail, each night as I laid in the dark, there would be one mosquito that had managed to get inside the net. It would not move until the light went out. I would hear it buzzing around my ear and all I could do was to wait for the damned thing to bite me so that I could go to sleep. Over time I was bitten by so many thousands of mosquitoes that I developed some sort of tolerance to the itching bites.

Father Henslemanns came to visit. His school was nearing

completion and he was having difficulty recruiting teachers. He asked if I would teach. I refused since I wasn't sent there to be

 a teacher. A few days later he returned again. I refused again. A few days more and he returned again. This time he asked me to come up and look at the school. I did and found the school to be most impressive – the only concrete and substantial structures in the entire valley. I offered him a deal. I would teach for half the day in any subjects he wished as long as I could teach an agriculture class. He didn't like this at all because this was not an authorized subject under the government standards. However he did accept this compromise and stuck to the agreement for as long as I was in Tambunan.

Teaching at St. Martin's Secondary School became by far the most satisfying thing I did in the Peace Corps. I went to the Dept. of Agriculture in Jesselton and found a British expatriate working at the higher levels. When I told him that I had managed to get agriculture into the school day (Sssssh. Don't tell anybody) he was very supportive. He agreed to supply baby chicks, an imported Australian hog and Talapia fish.

Much of the final work in constructing the school was done by its own students. They leveled fields, built a chicken coop, helped finish a fish pond and built a platform over the fishpond for the pig. The pig pooped and fed the fish. By the middle of the school year, the school produced eggs and fish for the boarding students to eat.

When the school opened the students were a real mix. The two elementary schools had produced a large number of kids with no place to continue. Hensey went through hundreds of applicants to select the small first class. Naturally he took the best and brightest. These kids were highly motivated and extremely intelligent. A few had to be my age. With the knowledge that there were a dozen kids waiting to take their place, discipline was not an issue. I hoped that they would not discover that most of them were smarter than their teacher.

Hensey was a smart politician and took in a certain number of kids from families connected to the 'system.' He kept most of them in a separate class because they could not compete with the much brighter students.

My first day was a long series of unexpected events. As I entered the first class, they all stood up and said, *"Good morning, Master!"* Shades of the ol' plantation! This rattled me completely. 'Master' was the usual form of address to any teacher. While it always amused me, it really meant nothing more.

They continued to stand. I told them to sit down. As I wrote my name on the blackboard, they all dutifully copied it into a notebook. I soon learned that they copied anything I wrote on the blackboard into a notebook. They were used to schools without textbooks and so made their own. If it was on the blackboard it was worth copying. I looked out over a class of about 40 kids. The room was neatly divided, boys on one side, girls on the other and a 'no man's land' in the center. I asked them to always sit in the same seat each day so that I could learn their names. I took out a paper to record their names. I asked the first boy in the first seat of the first row to tell me his name. He jumped up, stood at attention and gave me some long Latin name that I knew could not possibly be his real name. I wrote it down and moved on. The next boy stood up at attention and gave me another long name. I couldn't spell half of them. "Laurentius," " Justinian," "Scholastica" and so on. As a Catholic school, Hensey had given each of them one of these tongue twisters. To add to the confusion, they shed the names outside of school. If I went looking for them in the village, nobody had clue who I was looking for.

There was only one other Peace Corps Volunteer in Tambunan at the time. Jane Lieberman was an assigned teacher, living and working at the school. On the second or third day, she was teaching her new class. Suddenly they all stood up in a panic and charged toward her, screaming or yelling in Kadazan. She had visions of being attacked by crazed headhunters. She got carried out the door in the rush. She stood terrified outside until one of the students calmed down enough to tell her that a snake had crawled up a bicycle propped against the wall of her classroom and stuck its head through the open window. Spied by a girl sitting a few inches away, English forgotten, she screamed out the Kadazan word for snake and, well, you get the rest.

Many of the kids had a difficult time adjusting to me. They were adapted to the British system that emphasizes memorization. I would ask a question, the student would rise, look at the ceiling and give an answer word for word from the text. Sometimes I asked the devastating follow-up – *"What does that mean?"* This was not part of the usual system and it could make the poor student very uncomfortable. If they repeated the text perfectly, what exactly was my problem? Over time, I think most of them saw the value of understanding is greater than the value of just repeating.

They loved the Agriculture class! This was something with which they could relate. Shakespeare was study; rice was food, home and family. Hensey reviewed every test in every class before it was given. He looked at the first test I gave in Agriculture and told me that it was much too difficult. I agreed to throw out the results if they did poorly. The lowest score made was 96%.

These kids were a joy to teach. They were highly motivated,

hard working and most were very intelligent. It was, however, hard to get them to ask questions – actually, it was impossible at first. As they sat there wordlessly, the lack of feedback to me left me wondering if I was having any effect. I discussed it with Hensey.   He made me understand that they often went to elementary schools where the teacher might have only a grade or two more education than the level taught. Teachers did not want to 'lose face' when unable to answer questions and so discouraged them being asked.

No amount of encouragement resulted in questions until I stumbled across a good method. Sometimes I would make a statement that was outrageously wrong – *"All chickens are white."* At first I got blank stares or wall-eyed fidgeting but eventually one of the braver students couldn't stand it and would raise a hand. *"Excuse me, Master, but are ALL chickens white?"* Praised for catching me, it became a classroom game. It also leads to discussions of genetics and so on. Many of them did become comfortable asking questions.

Not everybody was happy with this. Hensey came to me and said that some of the other teachers had complained that I had taught the students to ask too many questions.

Sometimes I had to disappear in the middle of a class. I was not an authorized teacher. When government inspectors arrived unexpectedly, I had to flee while the class suddenly turned into a study hall or some other teacher stepped in. Some students asked me why they didn't get a grade in the agriculture class marked on their official transcripts. I designed a nice certificate indicating that a person had successfully completed a one year course in agriculture, sent it off to Patt Brett and received 200 copies back. When the District Agricultural Officer found out, he had a fit. I ignored him.

Each day of teaching had a different challenge. Some days were forever memorable. I'm teaching history or something when a hand went up in the back of the class. One of the girls had a question.

"Master, what is 'circumcision'?"

"Uh, why are you asking that in history class?"

"This word came up in Religion class. Father Henselmans told us to ask you."

He did, did he? Well, OK. I drew an obvious picture on the blackboard. As I began to talk about the religious ceremonies in some places, all eyes swiveled toward the one Muslim boy in the school. Fortunately these kids all knew what circumcision is, they just didn't know the English word.

The pig supplied to the school by the Ag Dept. had grown ever larger. They boys had constructed a very sturdy pen over the water of the fishpond but the pig liked to chew on the wood. As I'm teaching, a boy rushed into the class.

"Father Henslemanns sent me. The pig has fallen into the water and can't get out."

I pointed at several of the biggest boys and told them to follow me. Taking this a possibility for great fun, they stood up to join me – except one. I had pointed at the one Muslim boy. "Uh, not you." I pointed at another boy and we all took off for the pond. Naturally the rest of the class followed. The pig, probably weighing 400 lbs. by now, was indeed in the water and could not climb the steep banks. The boys jumped into the pond and were having great fun pushing the squealing pig up the bank but they were not having much success. It would struggle and slid back down the slick muddy bank. In the uproar soon the entire school lined the banks to cheer on the boys. Another half dozen jumped into the pond to help. Other boys ran to the pen with planks and nailed over the hole chewed by the pig.

By the time we got the pig out of the water and back into the pen, I had about 30 boys completely covered with black mud. I lined them up in a row and hosed each one off with a garden hose. School was finished for the day. I think it was the most fun they had all year.

A student hands me a note from a missing class member. "Dear Master, I cannot come to school today because I was drunk last night and am sick." I was shocked to get this from a 14 year old. It was an all too common problem – if there was a cultural problem, then tapai was it.

Tapai is brewed from rice, fermented in large jars. A substantial part of the annual rice production went to this use. It has a sour flavor and leaves a taste in the mouth somewhat like vomit. With little else to do in the evenings, competitive drinking is a pastime. A long straw is inserted into the jar clear down to the bottom. The first drinker, usually selected for capacity, sucks down the level as far as possible. A mark is made at the level and water carefully poured into the jar to bring the level back up to the top. The idea is to not mix this water with the tapai. The next drinker is expected to bring the level back down to the same or lower level. One round is usually sufficient to make everybody rip roaring drunk. The alcohol content is probably higher than wine but lower than hard liquor.

Lacking television, radio or other diversions, tapai is often the entertainment for the evening. There is no minimum age so that quite young children might be seen drunk and sprawled on the floor. To the Kadazan credit, they made good drunks, not belligerent or mean. I hated the stuff but it was unavoidable. Having eaten with the hosts and, on trips, sleeping in their house, to refuse to drink with them would be an affront. After drinking some of it, I might pretend to be drunk and try to go to sleep.

Bernard is about 16 and one of the boarders at the school. He is a bit of a free spirit, something not encouraged. On a Saturday afternoon, Bernard appears at my door, disheveled and quite drunk.

"Master, I must get back to the school now or Father Henslemanns will be very angry with me. Please take me on your motorcycle."

With Bernard clutching my waist and his head bouncing against my back, I haul him back to the school. Bernard's plan is to get back to the dormitory unnoticed and sleep it off.

Father Henslemanns is standing at the gate as I pass through. Naturally Bernard's goose is cooked now. I explain that he appeared at my door in this condition and I was just returning him to the school – no, I didn't get him into this condition. I leave Bernard to his fate.

On Sunday morning Bernard and his massive hangover appear again at my door. Hensey has thrown him out of the boarding dorm for two weeks but not out of school. Poor Bernard is half sick, totally frightened that he will be kicked out of school, too far from home to commute and a pariah to his classmates who fear guilt by association if they take him in. Can he stay? Sarus shrugs and Bernard gets a corner of the floor.

For two weeks at least Bernard is a model of behavior. He makes his way to our house each afternoon and throws himself into his books to study. Sarus does not keep tapai in his house nor does Bernard want any. I do feel sorry for him. His behavior is not acceptable by Hensey's standards, and rightly so. But short of never leaving the school, he also has little chance of refusing to drink.

Probably about 15, Sahadin is a quiet boy who says little. He walked the five or so miles from his village to go to school in spite of not having applied or been accepted. Hensey tells him to go home and try for enrollment next year. Each day Sahadin reappears with the same request. This goes on for about a week before Hensey gives in and enrolls him. He isn't a great student but works hard and asks for little. I'm sure that before he came to the school he had never seen an electric light. In a few weeks Sahadin is in charge of the small generator at the school. Each evening he coaxes it into life to provide lights for a few hours for the boarders and teachers. It is a leap of a thousand years and I wondered how he did it so quickly.

Sahadin is typical in other ways. Most of the students came from families that had little or no formal education and saw little value in it. They worked hard to stay in school without much support or encouragement from their families. Girls were sometimes actively discouraged. Each of them had some spark that drove them to keep at it. I asked a few of them what they planned to do in the future. Most of them had difficulty in articulating the reasons they kept at their studies and where they thought it would lead.

Peace Corps had a 'no exceptions' rule. If you got involved romantically or sexually with the people of Sabah, you were sent home. One of our group married just a few weeks after arriving and was sent home immediately. Although the Kadazans were not Muslims, the government was with all the Muslim sexual restrictions as policy. In this regard the Peace Crops was a hardship but I understood the policy and followed it

I still had responsibilities outside of the school. Paul (from the Ag office) and I traveled around the valley contacting farmers. If their crop of rice had problems we tried to assist. We had a strange act but it worked. Most of the time the farmers would ask me for solutions and ignore Paul. I still knew damned near nothing about agriculture while Paul was experienced and well trained. It was a continuation of the 'White men know everything' attitude. I'm glad that Paul had a good sense of humor and a sensible approach. We would both listen to the question from the farmer and I would repeat whatever Paul said. Me, the farmer would listen to – Paul, they would not.

One day I'm walking alone through a village and a farmer ran out of his padi field to corner me. He had some disease affecting his rice and wanted to know what to do. I looked at the rice and, surprise, was clueless. I tried to explain that I didn't know what the problem was but I would return the next day with Paul and we would do our best. The farmer became quite agitated and accused me of not wanting to help him. This lead to accusations that I did not like him – that had to be the only reason I would not tell him how to fix his crop. I ended up having to walk to town, find Paul and drag him back to the farmer's field on his day off.

Patty Bradford, a nurse from my Peace Corps training group, arrived in town. She had been assigned to another place but asked for a transfer when she found that she wasn't really needed. The local clinic staff had years of experience. She arrived in Tambunan while I was still living way out on the Ag Station so I rarely saw her. When she discovered that the staff of Tambunan's little clinic had worked under several earlier Peace Corps nurses – a repeat of her first assignment – she resigned from the Peace Corps and went home. She left me with a large supply of medicine from the Peace Corps.

As I traveled around the area, I found that health problems were far more common than rice problems. I also knew a lot more about medicine than I knew about rice. I began to carry a supply of medical supplies with me. It did not take long for me to realize that this was much more important than passing myself off as some sort of ag expert. It was difficult to starve in

Sabah with fruits and vegetables growing wild almost everywhere. It was much more likely to suffer from infections from cuts, simple diseases and parasites. The clinic staff did not travel about so I was not competing with them. On trips out of the valley to more isolated villages, I soon just dropped the pretense of being some agricultural expert.

Sometimes a student would invite me to their family home. Peter Ampong did so and it became a favorite trip. We had to cross a river back and forth too many times to count for about six hours to arrive at Monsok. The entire village showed up with their assorted cuts, headaches, belly aches and so on. I set up shop in the center of the village of perhaps 60 people. It took me awhile to catch on to the desire of perfectly healthy people to get some 'ubat' or medicine. They received mild aspirin so that nobody was offended. I did what I could for the others. I could not carry enough food for myself and the others that accompanied me but I always did carry some cans of highly prized foods like sardines or Chinese chicken. Canned goods required money to buy and so were not often seen in these remote places. I would contribute a can or two and receive a large meal in return. I knew better than to ask what I was eating. I'd already experienced meals of bat and monkey and felt better uninformed. As soon as the meal finished the damned tapai jugs appeared. In a large room with a lot of people, light by a single candle , I had no choice but to drink at least something of it. There would be no sleep until the drinking stopped. These villages were much poorer than those in the valley and perhaps that is the reason that the tapai drinking did not go on long. Not to mention that it was a 12 hour round trip walk to replace that candle. Soon Peter and I lay down on the floor, pulled sheets over ourselves and went to sleep.

The next day was a repeat of the first, except that we stayed in a small settlement of a few houses. On the fifth day we reached Monsok Ulu, Peter's home. His family was gracious and welcoming but I had great difficulty in really understanding just how different Peter's life was at school and here at home. This was really primitive living. How Peter found his way out of this life and into the school, and the motivation to do it, is astonishing. I could see that Peter was a bit lost; no longer completely at home here and not sure where he fit 'out there.' Or perhaps he was just caught between teacher and family.

Monsok Ulu was the end of the trail, just a few houses along the small river and miles to any school or medical help. There is no sign of crops or farming. In spite of the lush jungle, the soil is poor and fragile. Peter's family will burn off a few acres of forest, plant rice for a few years and then move on as the soil is exhausted. The forest will not recover for many years. They do not know that the value of the trees destroyed is probably 1000 times the value of the crops they grow. The rice crop is poor but sufficient. Fruits and vegetables grow wild everywhere.

This is triple canopy jungle. The ground is covered with dense growths of vines, ferns and low light plants. The second layer is the tops of trees such as banyans and mangroves. They often have massive trunks and are covered in parasitic bromeliads. The very tallest trees are well over 100 feet tall and shade the lower levels. On the sunniest days the walk through here is shaded and almost dark. The humidity is high. As usual, the trails are like highways to the people who live here and invisible to me. The trail follows the river that has often cut deep banks through the soil. We cross back and forth through the foot deep water dozens of time. The fast shallow current makes its

own noise as background to the calls of birds and monkeys, always unseen. There is the threat of snakes for Peter, who slides noiselessly through the growth. I suppose that he is safer with me as I crash through the leaves with enough noise to scare off anything.

I never know what to wear on these trips. The millions of land leaches are best handled with the almost bare feet of flip-flops and a cigarette. The hoards of mosquitoes can bite through a damp shirt stuck to the skin so I often do not wear one. The irritation from the leaves whipping my skin is only slightly less uncomfortable than sweltering and dripping in a shirt. My glasses fog up constantly. I need to be careful where I stop to rest. It is not wise to sit down in the jungle, providing new targets for the land leaches and bugs. Standing still attracts crawly things. I find the best rest is on a partially submerged rock in the swallow river. There are also huge water leaches but they are not in the swift current.

After this first trip with Peter, I will return to Monsok Ulu 5 or 6 more times. Word of this trek gets around and I have requests to make the journey with me from other volunteers and even a few strangers. I chose carefully among them because I do not want 'tourists' intruding on people I consider friends. Some of the students at the school are also interested; they grew up in the open valley. I invite several of them at a time to help carry medicine and canned food along with me.

Jane comes along on one trip along with Martin and Linus, two of the school students. Linus (above) is very short, even by local standards, but is very strong. Our guide to the first village is a kid about 8 years old. He will lead us for a day and then return home alone through the jungle. After a few hours, the rain begins, sometimes light and sometimes very heavy. The river begins to rise very quickly and the current ever stronger. At first it is knee-deep, then hip-deep and finally up to my armpits. We have no choice but to continue crisscrossing unless we wish to spend the night in the rain and jungle. Martin carries the tiny guide across. Poor Linus is now up to his neck but manages to keep his footing on the slippery bottom with the weight of his load held over his head.

Jane is upstream from Linus when she begins to float. If she goes out of sight we might never find her. She maneuvers in the direction of Linus. Now on a collision course, Linus braces himself against a boulder. Jane reaches him and wraps her legs around his middle. His face goes between her breasts. His arms are still holding his load above his head while Jane envelopes him with arms and legs. Over the rushing water I hear a muffled, *"Miss Jane, PUT your legs down!"*

Safe now, Jane is laughing loudly. Martin has developed an intense interest in his fingernails. I wish I had a waterproof camera. Linus continues to stand solid with Jane clamped around his middle and his face buried. I reach them where Linus and I manage to hold Jane's arms and get her to shore. Jane and I try not to laugh further. Poor Linus is incredibly embarrassed at the position he just had with – Oh, my God – his teacher. It will be some hours before he can look her in the eye again. Martin, perhaps knowing the consequences with Linus, never changes expressions.

On other trips I take Volunteers from other areas. I did once misjudge and took two young New Zealanders along. I warned them about the tapai but they were in for the maximum experience. They became so drunk in Monsok that I sent them back the next day with huge hangovers. They were unable to speak with anybody in the village so I told them they had no choice. I didn't want them on the rest of the trip and saw no reason why the people of Monsok needed to baby-sit them until I returned.

I think my visits were popular for the medicine I brought along. I could do little about the parasites giving the children their round bellies but did manage to stop a lot of infections from cuts and bites from growing much worse. People did in fact die from such simple things that were easy to treat with a little antibiotic cream. I saw the results of badly reset broken bones, untreated bad teeth and deep scars from who knows what. I could neither diagnose nor treat many things but people were always grateful for my efforts. I don't think I killed anybody with my aspirin or Bacitracin. In Peace Corps training I had been warned that I might be blamed for the death of a person I tried to unsuccessfully help. I saw no moral way to refuse doing what I did and, if I was blamed for anything, I never was aware of it.

Forget my role in the Agriculture Department! This slash and burn agriculture had been in practice for hundreds of years.

There was no flat land out here for other types of rice cultivation. It was estimated that it took 100 years for an abandoned rice plot to fully recover but the population out here was very low and I saw no alternatives. People out here did the best they could and I had nothing to offer to improve it.

My load of canned goods was more than an effort to contribute to the generosity of the people who fed and housed me on these trips. It was also self-defense. On my first trip with Peter, I sat in the large house with one tiny flickering candle for light. Dinner came in a large bowl with leaves and a few chunks of meat. I could barely see the bowl, much less the contents. It was, as so often was the case, neither good nor bad. It nourished but had little flavor. I spooned a chunk of meat into my mouth. It was round and tough so I chewed and chewed and chewed with little success in reducing its size. With this large lump moved to the side of my mouth I asked, *"Peter, what kind of meat is this?"*

"Bat."

"Bat?"

"Bat."

Hmm, what part of a bat is large and round? Discretely, I hoped, in the dark I spit out the chunk into my hand. I looked at it. And it looked at me. Too big to push through the bamboo floor and certainly not going back into my mouth, I stuck it into my pocket. Later, out for an evening pee, it disappeared into the river. From then on I made sure to have a lot of canned sardines to be shared at meals. I never again asked what I was eating until the meal was finished.

Around this time the Peace Corps in Malaysia tried an interesting experiment. They were aware that the standard salary for Volunteers in urban areas was inadequate and probably more than needed in places like Tambunan. On a strictly "no questions asked" basis each of us was asked to adjust our salary to any level we thought appropriate. Like many I adjusted mine down a bit. It was too little to think about saving for the future in any case but more than adequate for my needs. In the end, the Peace Corps staff reneged on their policy and questioned two salary requests. One Volunteer in Sarawak reduced his salary to a ridiculous level. When they did investigate, it turned out that he was a premier moocher who sponged all his meals off of his neighbors. The other was Larry Duffy, at 60 the oldest Volunteer from my group. He asked for about US$600 a month. When asked why he needed so much, he responded, *"Don't you know what a bottle of Scotch costs in this country?'*

I had been around for many births. Perhaps as a defense, most babies didn't receive a name for a few months just in case they didn't make it. Death was another story. In the two years I was in Tambunan obviously people died. I never saw or heard of a burial or funeral. Death and dead people were greatly feared and apparently disposed of quickly and quietly. Houses where people had died, especially in cases of suicide, were sometimes abandoned. The dead were rarely mentioned. The fear of huntus (ghosts) was universal and great. Burial grounds were rarely entered during the day and never at night! I sometimes walked through the Chinese burial grounds between town and my house in the evenings to prove a point. My friends would detour a longer route and eventually told me that the local huntu only bothered local people.

The time passed quickly in the Peace Corps. Surrounded by accepting and welcoming people, I truly did feel at home here. In spite of the lack of electricity, plumbing and roads, life was easy, the climate perfect and the offered friendships genuine. Like many Volunteers I could have stayed on much longer. The Peace Corps and the Malaysian government perhaps recognized this and did not allow extensions. With the end of my two years approaching, I had to think of the future.

Near the end of tours the Peace Corps sent out a monthly letter with job possibilities listed. I had no idea what I wanted to do but I did know that Oklahoma was definitely not where I wanted to go. I read through the lists but found little of interest. English teachers were needed in Turkey but I saw no reason to work for the $150 a month offered. Everything else looked boring and dull after the Peace Corps.

Only one listing looked even remotely interesting. The Agency for International Development – an agency I had never heard of – needed people with unusual qualifications to work overseas. They wanted university graduates with degrees in psychology or sociology, a proven ability to speak a foreign language and at least one year living overseas (the military did not count for this). These requirements must have reduced the pool of qualified applicants to a small number. And they paid well.

I sent them a letter expressing interest. A few weeks later I received a reply offering to give me an interview in Washington, DC, at my convenience. I accepted their offer and noted that it would be months before I arrived home. No problem!

Leaving Tambunan was an emotional event. The school held a party and dance, Father Henslemanns was gracious in his speech and a string of students made flowery but heartfelt speeches that I found difficult to listen to and remain composed. Many of these young people were more than students, they were friends.

I decided to leave Tambunan, not by Land Rover and train, but by one last trek through the jungle. With my one suitcase slung on a bamboo pole and carried by two of the students, we headed out. The road had reached a point where the trip no longer took two days. We reached the road in the early afternoon to find the Land Rover to Jesselton parked and waiting. One last long goodbye and the vehicle began to move. I watched my friends disappear back into the trees.

I met many of my Peace Corps group in Jesselton as we all were leaving about the same time. A medical exam, a trip to the dentist and a ticket home in hand and it was over.

Peace Corps did not like volunteers to linger overseas. Our salary – a grand $900 for two years work – would be in the form of a check sent to our home address. I arranged for my father to send me the $900 in advance and I had saved a little of my living expenses. There wasn't much to buy in Tambunan. I traded my Peace Corps ticket at the local travel agency for a much longer trip home – Singapore, Thailand, Ceylon, India, Nepal, Afghanistan, Russia, Egypt, Greece, Italy, Switzerland, Austria, Germany and Holland. Pat Brett, the secretary, Sandy Deukmajian and Linda Ledbetter, both nurses, and I would meet in Rome. Sandy's father was a car dealer in California and would arrange for Sandy to have a new Volkswagen waiting in Rome. We would drive around Europe and then I would continue from Amersterdam on to Washington for my interview and then home.

The trip home took months and I fulfilled the requirements to travel this way. I was young, poor and foolish. In 1969 the world was a safer place but not that safe. I stayed in cheap hotels in bad areas, ate in questionable restaurants and traveled around in buses and taxis not usually used by foreigners. This trip alone could fill a book but I will spare the reader more than just a few stories.

That damned draft board? I lost my deferment the day I left Sabah. I fulfilled the law to the letter. At each hotel where I stayed over the next months I sent my favorite draft board secretary a post card to tell her my new address. I saw no reason to spend the money on air mail so they arrived out of order and many weeks after I sent them.

The four of us met in Singapore. After a few days of touring the place, we dispersed. I went on to Bangkok. I ran across Art Eith, a member of our group, staying at the same cheap hotel so we decided to look around together.

We toured the huge temple complex in central Bangkok. For lunch we found a tent cafeteria set up in the large open field nearby. Nobody spoke English. We joined the line and received a large tray of food. There was no cash register at the end of the steam tables. We had taken our food from a welfare organization feeding the poor! We were acutely embarrassed but thought that abandoning the trays of food would be even more embarrassing so we found a table, ducked our heads and were eating in silence. Nobody seemed to mind.

Two saffron-robed monks approached. One was about our age and the other older. The younger monk asked us, in very good English, *"May we join you?"* They sat down at our table before we could answer. The younger monk prattled on nonstop in English. The other monk never said a word. After a good half-hour of nonstop commentary on the weather, the temples,

Bangkok, traffic, his health, our health and so on, the older monk rose, nodded to the younger, and left, still without a word. The younger monk remained but visibly relaxed and mercifully finally shut up.

"What is this all about?" asked Art.

"I'm sorry," he said. *"The other monk is my English teacher and you were my final exam. So sorry to talk so much but I was afraid that if you talked to me I might not understand so I just kept talking!"* Would we like him to show us around? Sure!

He was an interesting fellow. The 13th child of a poor family, he had literally been given to the monastery when he was 6 years old. The monks fed, educated and raised him. His English training had been ordered by the head monk who felt that the large numbers of American troops from Viet-Nam needed monks to guide them through the temples and explain Buddhism.

He stayed with Art and me for the rest of the day, even following us back to the hotel. Art and I were taking the train to Chingmai the next day. The monk offered to go with us. We explained that we really didn't have enough money to buy him a ticket. *"Oh, monks travel for free on the trains."* Sure, why not?

We met again at the train station the next morning. The schedule showed the train leaving at 8 in the morning and arriving at 6 in the evening. We bought third class tickets with the monk's help and climbed aboard. The monk just followed and, sure enough, was never asked for a ticket. The train was not crowded but the wooden seats were not very comfortable. The train pulled out and very slowly made its way through the countryside. After a few hours, I commented that I would be glad to get off the train and have a good dinner in a comfortable chair. The monk looked puzzled. *"The train arrives at 6 o'clock tomorrow night."* Unfortunately he was correct. Underweight at 120 lbs. my boney butt was paralyzed and bruised by the time we arrived. It remains one of the most uncomfortable nights I have ever spent.

When we finally arrived in Chingmai, Art and I decided to look for a cheap hotel. The monk had another idea. He invited us to stay at a monastery for free. This fit our budget much better. He took us off to a place near the center of town and introduced us to the head monk. We were offered a place to sleep at the feet of a large golden Buddha in the main temple. In return we were asked to help the temple's younger monks with English pronunciation.

I was used to sleeping on the floor but had never slept on an altar with a 10 foot Buddha staring down on me. On the second evening I returned from taking a bath with a towel wrapped around me. The monk wanted help with some text in his English book. As we talked, Art lifted my camera and took a picture. Forty years and 15,000 photos later, my favorite photo is one that I did not take.

We saved enough money on the hotel to rent a car for the day. The villages around Chingmai all have one industry each. One does silver, one made umbrellas, another wove cloth. It was an interesting side trip. We climbed the endless stairs up to the King's summer palace. When it was time to move on, we made sure that we bought tickets on the faster train back to Bangkok. We went directly from the train station to the airport with the monk still on our tail. I thought he might decide to just continue on to the USA with us.

The Bangkok airport is quite far from town so Art and I thought that we had to give the monk enough money for the taxi ride back to the city. Monks do not accept money. He had an easy solution. *"I'll turn around and if you just place it in my bag while I'm not looking, then I haven't accepted anything."*

Art went his own way while I continued on the Ceylon. I toured the country mostly by train, meeting a lot of interesting people and seeing a lot of temples and stupas.

I flew from Ceylon to Calcutta. On the plane to Calcutta I sat next to a French photographer for Paris Match magazine. He had a car arranged to take him around the city to make photographs for the magazine. Would I like to accompany him? Sure! I thought I was prepared for almost anything but the poverty, filth and despair of Calcutta were difficult to take. He hadn't told me that he was looking for the worst possible photos for the magazine. He would stop the car, get out, and stick his camera in the faces of people in the worst circumstances – dying, starving, diseased, crippled. He invited me to take similar photos. I couldn't do it and was glad to see the last of him at the end of the day.

Another day in Calcutta on my own was more than enough. I continued on to Nepal. By the time I arrived in Nepal I had a medical problem. I bought a pair of shoes in Singapore but they had worn a large blister on my heels. This was no doubt the result of no shoes for several years. Not sure what to do, I went to the Peace Corps office where the Peace Corps doctor kindly treated the problem even though I was no longer in the Peace Corps. In the office I met a Nepal Peace Corps Volunteer being treated for internal parasites. He had to stay in town for a few days until his treatment was finished. Would I like him to show me around? Sure!

He showed me temples covered in pornographic art. (Now there is a religion with a 'broad' appeal.) He also showed me examples of religious tolerance that the rest of the world should follow. In one temple the Hindus held services in the morning and the Buddhists in the afternoon. I saw the Living Goddess – a young girl worshipped as a deity until puberty. Then she is thrown out of the temple to fend for herself. He also directed me to a decent hotel with a price I have never again equaled. A room was 10 cents US a day with a bicycle thrown into the deal. Nepal was a place I wished to revisit again.

At the airport I sat next to a middle-aged American who struck up a conversation. He was a professor ending a five year contract in India at an Indian university. His wife and family had left for the States and he was making one last tour of India alone. Would I like to join him on a road trip from the east coast of India down to the southern tip and up the west coast to Bombay? Sure!

He had a car and driver. Southern India proved to be green, uncrowded and much less poor. We toured religious and cultural sites, rented a canoe for a river trip complete with a young boy to paddle. It helped offset the impressions of Calcutta. I saw the Sky People, a religious group that believes all clothing is evil and who wander the streets as families completely naked. I watched young men climb up tall coconut trees to drink todai, a potent brew allowed to ferment in the tree. They went up sober and came down drunk. Some of them, I'm sure, came down quicker than others.

We stayed in government rest houses. Built by the British, they provided foreigners a decent place to stay in almost every town at a very cheap price.

It took several weeks to reach Bombay and time was running out for me to meet Sandy, Pat and Linda in Rome. I decided to skip Afghanistan. I spent several days visiting the Russian Embassy for a visa. They turned me down. Well, at least I had more time for other destinations.

I boarded Air India for Cairo, Egypt. This is a long flight and it turned out they forgot to pack meals. I arrived hungry and tired. At the airport in Cairo I located a free bus to the Nile Hilton. One look at the lobby and I knew I could not afford it so I left my one bag there and walked around the surrounding area until I found a cheap hotel about a block away.

As I checked in the clerk insisted that he needed to keep my passport. He explained that all foreigners needed to register their passports at the local police station and that either I let him do it or I could do it myself – but don't expect any English at the Police Station. Reluctantly I let him take my passport.

I spent the day in the famous Cairo Museum and the incredible display of King Tut's artifacts. Most of the displays were surrounded by tons of sandbags because the Israelis had bombed the city recently. After hours of wandering around the place I finally located the famous solid gold coffin of Tut. Well, I located the place where it should have been. The display case had a small sign on it – Removed for security purposes.

When I returned to the hotel in the late afternoon I asked for my passport. The clerk looked nervous and said that I needed to go to the Police Station myself to get it. He gave me directions and off I went. At the station there was a policeman who spoke English. I was directed to sit down and wait. And wait I did. After several hours I began to get agitated and demanded my passport. This time I was told to sit down and shut up. I threatened to call the American Embassy. *"Your Embassy is closed. Egypt and America do not have diplomatic relations right now."* Ooops.

I sat in the police station all night, unable to leave. In the early morning the police apparently decided that they had made some point, gave me my passport and let me go. I went back to my hotel, where the clerk at least had the courtesy to look a bit relieved to see me, and collapsed for a few hours sleep. I was not getting a good impression of Egypt.

In the afternoon I went to the Cairo market and met some of the most disagreeable people on earth. Shopkeepers would invite me into their shops, give me coffee or a soft drink, and bring out their wares. If I did not buy something they screamed filthy threats in English and Arabic. If I did not go into their shops, they ranted. I didn't stay long.

On the third day I decided to walk over to the Hilton to look for more friendly people, perhaps other tourists. At the desk I asked about trips out to the Pyramids. Standing behind me was a couple on the same mission. He introduced himself in broken English and asked if I would like to join them in renting a car and driver for a day-long trip around Cairo and out to the Pyramids. Sure!

The Polish colonel and his wife were in Egypt as part of the Soviet team building the Aswan Dam. She spoke no English. The three of us spent the day crawling over and in the pyramids before heading back to the city. Some distance from the pyramids, the colonel asked the driver to stop so that he could take a photo. As he stood by the side of the road with his camera, a large Army truck carrying a tank passed by. A following truck full of soldiers immediately stopped, convinced that the colonel was taking photos of military equipment. I quickly threw my camera under the driver's seat. We were ordered to follow the truck with an armed solider squeezed into the car with us.

We spent a couple of hours at a Military Police Station while the colonel got the mess straightened out. They took his film but returned his camera. They did not discover my camera still under the car seat. The driver was terrified.

Egypt may be full of interesting things to see but I had my fill of the place by the time we got back to the Hilton. "Arrested" twice in two and a half days was enough. I went to the travel desk and booked myself out on the first flight to Greece the next morning.

Ah, Greece! What a change from Egypt and Asia. I found a cheap hotel on the edge of town. It was comfortable and clean and had a good restaurant. Unfortunately the small beautiful garden behind my room also had a few peacocks that tuned up very early in the morning but you can't have everything. Down the street was a small store where I bought a small loaf of bread and a liter of cold milk – something I had not had for two years. I sat on the curb and drank the milk and ate the bread. God, it was good! I sat on the curb and threw up the milk and bread. It would be months before I could digest dairy products again.

I rented a Volkswagen Beetle from the hotel and drove to the southern tip of Greece. On the way back I picked up two hitch-hiking middle aged ladies headed for Athens. They spoke no English so they sang at the top of their lungs for the rest of the trip. They sang well and it was a nice gesture.

Standing on a street corner, somebody tapped me on the shoulder. I turned to see Cathy O'Brian, a nurse from my Peace Crops group. Small world. She and I traveled together to Delphi. We took a ferry to Mikonos and Delos. Nobody lived on Delos and it was strictly a day trip by small boat. Cathy and I were warned that there was no place to eat or drink so we went prepared. We bought the makings for few sandwiches and some bottles of what appeared to be red soda pop. We threw the sodas into the cold sea water when we arrived at the island and went off touring. By lunch we were both more thirsty than hungry. The boat we hired for the round trip did not wait so we had a few hours to lie in the sun and have a leisurely lunch. We both quickly drank three of the sodas before eating. They had a peculiar flavor, not unpleasant but not very good. This was my introduction to the Greek Retsina, a weak wine flavored mostly with turpentine. We both developed splitting headaches before napping on the beach for about an hour. I can't stand the stuff to this day. After returning to Mykonos, we ate in a small tavern where the men lined up and danced together a la Zorba.

On the agreed upon day, I flew to Rome and met Sandy, Pat and Linda on the Spanish steps. Sandy already had the car her father arranged and had rooms for us at a small home nearby, run by an old lady. She spoke no English and we spoke no Italian. On the afternoon of the second day she took my bag out of my room and dumped it in the living room. After a great deal of shouting and hand waving, we figured out that she had rented my room to somebody else for the day. I would get it back that evening.

Traveling with three women sounded great. It was something less. Stuffed into a tiny car with more luggage than I thought possible, we were all paralyzed by the end of the day. Driving the overloaded chugging car through the Alps, large buses blew their horns for us to get out of the way. At each stop we looked like circus clowns crawling out of one of those miniature cars. The three of us had a great time touring Italy, Switzerland, Austria and Germany but the trip was costing me three times as much as the others. We stayed in small pensions where the three women shared a room while I paid for mine alone. Finally, in Munich I was down to $20. I had no choice but to book my flight to Washington, DC, for a few days with friends while I had the interview with the Agency for International Development. The three women traveled on.

In Washington, I stayed with Craig, one of the staff at my Peace Corps training two years earlier. I called the number at A.I.D. and arranged the interview.

It was a strange interview. I thought somebody must have done a lot of homework on me since they asked no questions about experience or qualifications. They did ask a lot of questions about my feelings and opinions about the Viet-Nam war. I truthfully told them that I had spent the last almost three years in a place with no radio, television or newspapers. Would I be willing to work in Viet-Nam? Yes. Could I write unbiased reports? I said that I knew the difference between facts and opinions. The interview lasted for several hours but at the end I was offered a job. Based upon my 'qualifications' – not explained – I was offered a beginning position one step above the usual entry level. They refused to be very precise in describing exactly what they wanted me to do. I accepted anyway. They told me that I would need to learn to speak Vietnamese and that I would start based on an opening in the language program.

I told them that the draft board classified me as 1-A. I didn't think that I would be available if there was to be any delay in hiring me. They gave me a letter addressed to the draft board. "The President of the United States has determined that it is in the best interests of the United States that this person not be called for military service." I needed to go home and wait until called by A.I.D.

I arrived home and waited a few days before personally delivering my letter to the draft board. When I entered the office, that same old prune stood behind the desk.

"Hello, I'm Cary Kassebaum."

Her reaction was immediate. *"You're that son of a bitch with all the post cards!"*

"Yep. And I've got one more for you." I handed her my letter. As she read it, her face turned deep red. Without a word she turned around and stomped off. I couldn't resist – *"Thanks for all your help."*

I remained 1-A for the next ten years but it didn't matter. Well, almost. I needed some job for the months before I started working in Washington. No matter where I went, as soon as they saw "1-A" on the application – and they all asked the question – I was given no further consideration.

I was finally reduced to applying at 7-11 for a job as a stock checker. The man in charge asked me why a college graduate wanted this kind of work. I truthfully explained that I needed something for a few months only. He told me that he had people everyday who claimed that their only goal in life was to work at 7-11. Then they would disappear without notice. He made me an offer. If I promised to give him two weeks' notice, he would hire me. Done.

Working for the Government

I finally received notice to report to the Agency for International Development in the State Department in Washington on December 26, 1969 – the day after Christmas. I gave 7-11 a full month's notice. My family had Christmas on December 23 so that I would have time to drive to Washington.

The drive was terrible with heavy snow for almost the entire trip. I arrived late on Christmas day and went directly to the hotel booked for me by the State Department. I still didn't have much money and was worried that this organization of diplomats would book me into some place I could not afford.

The Allen F. Lee Hotel is across the street from the State Department. I should not have worried. It is a dump. I had a room in the basement with a tiny window at ground level, now covered by snow. Nothing was open so I went without dinner.

At 9 o'clock in the morning I went across the street to report in. The building was almost deserted. When I finally found the right office all of the desks were empty except one. I introduced myself. The lady behind the desk looked surprised. *"Why are you here today?"*

"Because this is the date I was asked to be here."

"Well, yes, but I didn't really expect you to be here today. Come back on January 2nd."

So much for busting my ass to drive half way across the United States in a snow storm to arrive as asked. The only good thing about it all was that she promised to have me on the payroll from December 26. I went back to my dingy hotel and spent the next week alone. I did not have any friends now in Washington, almost everything was closed and the weather remained awful.

On the day after the New Year's holiday I reported in again. I spent the day filling out endless forms that each went to a different office, setting up a bank account for my pay to be deposited, getting ID cards and an Official passport.

I worked for the Agency for International Development for exactly one day.

CORDS

By the end of the day I had been hired, I was seconded ("lent") to CORDS. CORDS stood for Combined Operations for Rural Development Support, about as meaningless a name as the government could create. I was immediately posted to Saigon. I thought this strange until I realized that it let me receive per diem (travel expenses) for the entire year I would be 'temporarily' working in Washington.

History lesson

What was CORDS? First we need to look at the Viet-Nam War. The United States had been involved in the fighting since, believe it or not, 1946. After World War II the French planned to reclaim its colony of Indochina. President Truman was not in favor of this but chose not to have a direct confrontation with France. He secretly provided some military assistance and American advisors to Ho Chi Minh, an avowed nationalist who kept his Communist leanings to himself.

By 1952, Ho Chi Minh's forces cornered the French Army in Dien Binh Phu and all but slaughtered them. The French pulled out leaving two new countries, North and South Viet-Nam. Both immediately became dictatorships with Ho Chi Minh declaring a Communist People's Republic of North Viet-Nam while the South declared a Republic supposedly democratic but falling under a series of petty dictators. Ho Chi Minh was determined to reunite Viet-Nam into one country and started a low level insurgency in the South. With Ho Chi Minh now openly Communist, Presidents Truman, Eisenhower, Kennedy and Johnson now supported the South with funds and supplies at low levels.

By the early 1960's the war began to heat up and it looked as if Ho Chi Minh might take over the South. President Johnson believed in the domino theory – if the Communists took over South Viet-Nam, they would continue on to Cambodia,

Thailand, Malaysia and so on. He needed a good reason to invade South Viet-Nam but recognized that the majority of Americans and Congress would not support this. Lacking a good reason, Johnson did what several Presidents before him, and certainly after, have done. He fabricated one.

He declared that the U.S. Navy, in international waters off the coast of South Viet-Nam, had been attacked by the North Vietnamese. An American destroyer did have a few bullet holes and no casualties. Most likely the damage was done at the orders and cooperation of the South Vietnamese who did have a good reason to want to involve the U.S. This "attack" made absolutely no sense, of course. The war was going well for Ho Chi Minh and the last thing he needed was to involve the superpower United States. In the uproar of the supposed attack, Johnson managed to get Congress and the majority of Americans to support giving him war powers. The U.S. invaded South Viet-Nam with troops to support the South Vietnamese Army.

The war quickly went from a low level insurgency supported by the North to a serious war involving the North Vietnamese Army for the first time. By 1969 the U.S. had over 200,000 troops in Viet-Nam. We were not winning and stuck in a situation that became very unpopular at home. Democrat Johnson declined to run for re-election and Republican Nixon replaced him.

The President received reports from three different sources in

Viet-Nam; the military filtered through the Pentagon, the Saigon Embassy filtered through the State Department and the CIA filtered through Langley. Each of these agencies had a lot of good people who made honest reports. But by the time they were combined and filtered through the system, they often changed. Nixon soon realized that the three sources rarely agreed and usually were self-serving to the reporting agency. From these reports it appeared that the military rarely lost, the South Vietnamese government was competent and honest and our spy network knew everything in advance. And yet we were losing.

My career and CORDS were funded by the CIA but the CIA had no control over any of it. Like it or not – mostly not – the CIA paid my salary, supplied my vehicles and furniture and promoted me when ordered to do so. At any one time, I doubt that there were more than 100 people in CORDS. It was a tiny and mostly unnoticed government agency.

Nixon wanted independent reporting and he created CORDS as the mechanism. He ordered the various Foreign Service agencies to take a small number of new hired people and second them to CORDS immediately (By law, civil servants cannot be posted overseas.). My colleges came from A.I.D., State, U.S.I.A. and the Foreign Commercial Service, all of us without a day's experience in our hiring agencies. We were expected to become fluent in Vietnamese and write clear unbiased reports for the White House on subjects assigned and as we thought worth submitting. Our reports went directly to the White House unseen by the military, State or CIA. Even the small bureaucracy of CORDS did not see them. Of course I knew none of this as I reported for my first day of work. At this point all I knew was that I had been hired to "work in Viet-Nam."(End)

I reported to the Vietnam Training Center located in the basement of a shopping center in Rosslynn, Virginia. It is gone now, replaced by the USA Today building. From 8 to 10 in the morning, we had a variety of sessions on Vietnamese culture, government, history, ethics and religions. About 90% of the people attending these sessions were Army officers destined to be Advisors to the Vietnamese military. Most of them looked as if they might actually die of boredom. We few generally young civilians stuck out prominently in the sea of uniforms. At times we had sessions just for those of us designated as 'reporters.' Several of these sessions were held by Secretary of State Henry Kissinger – an indication of the priority Nixon gave to the program. From 10 to 6 in the evening it was Vietnamese language. The military saw no need for their advisors to speak Vietnamese and they did not attend. Each class had no more than 5 CORDS people in it, with a fresh instructor each hour. The total course was 52 weeks of this for 5 days each week without a break. It was physically and mentally exhausting. The entire year is just a blur now.

The Center had an interesting policy. Each 6 weeks we took an oral exam in Vietnamese. Those who passed stayed on for the next 6 weeks. Those who did not were sent to Viet-Nam as paper-pushers for the Embassy. Most were let go after their two year contract expired. Of the 5 people I started with, I was the only person to complete the entire course. Even I was surprised to find that I was good at it.

I also spent two weeks at the Special Forces school in North Carolina learning scary things like wiring plastic C-4 bombs and booby traps, firing rocket launchers and setting Claymore mines. When I (well, we) asked why these skills were required, the answer was 'just in case.' We also spent each evening for a month at the International Police Academy in Georgetown. We were each issued a 38 cal. short barreled pistol and spent a lot of time at target practice. These pistols are accurate for about 6 feet but make a hell of a hole.

Viet-Nam

Pistol in my pocket (Yes, there were times then when you could do that.), I boarded PanAm for the flight to Saigon. I needed a break after the past year and so booked myself to Saigon via Samoa, Tahiti, Fiji, New Zealand, Australia, Singapore and Sabah. It cost me about $200 extra. I didn't have enough vacation time accrued for 5 week trip but the office made it clear that they didn't care. (It took me awhile before I figured out that my Vietnamese fluency earned a lot of informal perks. Although about 1 ½ million Americans served in Viet-Nam, slightly less than 200 were ever considered fluent in Vietnamese and we were not all in the country at the same time.)

We were still at about 30,000 feet when the pilot announced that we would be landing in Saigon in a few minutes. The Boeing 747 went into a tight spiral at a very steep angle to avoid exposure to missile fire. It was, for me, the first concrete evidence and realization that I really was going into a war zone. Before we landed I suddenly had misgivings about this job. It didn't help that the sudden change in pressure made my head feel as if it would explode.

I was met by a young Vietnamese man who spoke good English. He took my bag to a waiting car and handed me a thick envelope. In a few minutes we were at a hotel where he left me and disappeared. After checking in and finding my room, I opened the envelope. Inside were a thick wad of Vietnamese money and a note telling me that a car would pick me up the next morning and take me to a flight to Can Tho. I had eaten on the plane and was very tired so I went to bed early.

Around midnight I awoke to a tremendous explosion from a rocket fired into the city. It missed the hotel but the explosion blew out the window at the end of the hall. Tired or not, I didn't get much sleep from that point on. Through all of the past year the war had been an abstraction for me. Some of my training had been 'war games' and it had often seemed to be a game to me. This was the first time that it really sank in that there actually were people out there who would like to kill me. This should not have come as a shock but it did.

I flew to Can Tho on a small single engine Air America plane that held one pilot and three passengers. It was too noisy to talk. At the Can Tho U.S. military airport I was again met by a young man who took me to 'Palm Springs,' an American housing compound. It had a small guest house where I was installed. There was a note on the bed telling me that John Paul Vann, the civilian commander of IV Corps, would meet with me "at his convenience" to discuss my assignment.

History lesson

John Paul Vann was one of the most famous people to come out of the Viet-Nam war. He is the subject of a book and movie; both titled *"A Bright, Shining Lie."* As a Lt. Col. in the Army, he had clashed with his superior officers over the conduct of the war. He quit the Army and returned as a CORDS civilian now commanding many of the officers with whom he clashed earlier. Hated by many, admired by many and worshipped by a few, I thought he was a very strange person. He was tiny at about 5' 4" but had an ego that more than made up for height. He had absolute faith that the war would be won and that the Vietnamese military could do it. Arrogant and uninterested in any ideas but his own, he demanded and rewarded absolute loyalty to his ideas and was vicious to any person who might disagree. He liked to wear Major-General's stars on the shoulders of his civilian shirts and demanded that all military under his command treat him with the deference and courtesy due a General. He expected to be saluted and that all would rise when he entered the room. He could, and did, ruin the careers of military officers who did not treat him as he desired.

To his credit he did push, cajole and inspire the Vietnamese to accomplish much more than they had in the past. Nonetheless, I thought he looked like a silly Bantam rooster strutting around in his own chicken yard. After my first meeting with him, I commented to a person in the hallway, *"Is this guy for real?"* I got a look of true distress and fear.

Fortunately for me, Vann transferred to I Corps at the other end of the country before he had a chance to discover how I felt about him. He was killed in a helicopter a few months later. (end)

(Note: There were so many factions and groups operating in Vietnam – no less than four different South Vietnamese Armies, the North Vietnamese, the Viet Cong, etc. that I will refer to all who supported the South Vietnamese effort as "Vietnamese" and all who supported the downfall of the South Vietnamese regime as "Viet Cong.")

I heard nothing from Vann the next day. I did have the chance to meet the Can Tho CORDS people in the evening because they all lived in this compound. On the third day, having heard nothing from Vann again, I walked over to his office. I was told to wait until he decided to see me and that it might be any hour of the day or night.

Around 10 in the morning of the fourth day, a breathless messenger arrived at the compound. *"Mr. Vann will see you NOW!"* I walked over to his office and was shown in right away. Vann had no desire for chitchat. He told me that he was sending me to spend a day and night in three different provinces. When I returned I was to give him my impressions of each. Dismissed! I think the only word I got in was *"Hello."*

His staff gave me a few minutes to gather my things at the compound and drove me back to the airport. A Huey helicopter was waiting for me with its engine running. My own personal helicopter – now this was cool! They delivered me to Rach Gia province located on the coast next to Cambodia.

The staff there spent the day doing their best to fill me in on the situation there and the problems they experienced. I met the CORDS person who was second in command of the U.S. military and civilian activities in the province. He was about my age. The CORDS guy had been in Rach Gia for about two years and, like me, was a Vietnamese speaker. With the average military tour in Viet-Nam being about 11 months, he had already seen three province U.S. military commanders.

I went on later to Bac Lieu and An Xuyen provinces, again in my private chopper. In each I thought the CORDS people were good, solid, sensible people who knew a great deal about the place they worked.

When I returned to Can Tho, Vann saw me immediately. He had few questions. *"Which province do you see as most secure?"*

"Rach Gia."
"Why?"

I explained in some detail that I saw it as the best organized, most prosperous and most secure. He listened without comment.

"Which is the least secure?"

"An Xuyen."

"Why?"

I gave him my reasons. When I finished, he said, *"I'm posting you to An Xuyen."* Dismissed!

The next day my really cool personal chopper took me back to Ca Mau, the capitol of An Xuyen Province. I was taken by Jeep to the Quang Long District headquarters to join, for 6 weeks, the U.S. Advisory Team to the District Chief. I was simply to observe. The six man team, headed up by a Major, 'advised' the Vietnamese. Home was a triangular shaped mud fortress with a concrete bunker/home. A small barracks, wooden and completely exposed, held a few bunks. I had been advised not reveal that I understood Vietnamese.

When I arrived in An Xuyen, the Viet Cong completely controlled about 70% of the land area of the province. About 20% of the province was Viet Cong by night and Vietnamese by day. The remaining 10% was firmly in Vietnamese hands. Because most of the population lived in Ca Mau and a few other sizable villages, however, the Vietnamese controlled most of the population. The French had built a series of low dikes that kept the salt water out of the rice producing areas. The war and neglect had destroyed them so that a huge area of formerly productive farm land was useless and abandoned. Only the northern areas of the province, where the city was located, remained productive. Many, if not most, of the people in the

Viet Cong areas lived as fishermen in the rivers and coastal area. I was unable to visit the vast majority of places in the province.For the first few days I followed the Major around and listened. My major function on this team was to take up space. As an observer, I had no real function. The team was aware that I would end up as one of their supervisors and so treated me well. The District Chief supposedly spoke English but I noted that he often misunderstood the Major. The District belonged to the South Vietnamese during the day and the Viet Cong at night. Right away I could see why this would be a difficult war. The South wore uniforms, built forts and operated like an Army. The Viet Cong spent their days as farmers or tradesmen. At night they attacked the Army. When not fighting they were virtually undetectable. The Viet Cong chose when and where to fight. The South could do little more than react.

On my third night with the team, we were attacked. Bullets, tracers, mortars and rockets were fired back in the general direction of the attack. The team jumped out of bunks and headed for the bunker. All of us were wearing only underwear, except the major  who augmented his outfit with a steel pot, combat boots and a pistol. The concrete bunker had a small battery powered light. The major flipped it on to light up a large snake in the center of the bunker. Talk about between a rock and a hard spot! Almost without thinking the Major did a Mexican hat dance on the snake with his boots and we all crowded in. The bunker had thousands of mosquitoes. Outside the fighting went on for about 45 minutes.

After it ended, I went back to bed and, strangely, immediately fell into a deep sleep. Or maybe the mosquitoes had just drained me of all blood.

The next morning the Major and I, the District Chief and some troops went out to assess the results of the fight. We found three really messed up dead people in a rice padi. There were no weapons. The Major counted three dead Viet Cong. The District Chief, claiming that if there were three bodies, the enemy probably carried off at least five more, decided to report 8 dead Viet Cong. I asked both the Major and the District Chief how they knew that these were not three farmers caught in the cross fire. The Major responded quite logically, *"I don't. And you don't know that they are farmers."*

Later counting the dead became my second worst duty. I found it much worse to count the wounded. There is a sensory overload in counting the dead. At first I wondered about these people, their families and their history. I stopped wondering. Viet Cong bodies were rarely claimed; to do so would place the family under suspicion. The dead carried no identification. They were displayed in neat rows for me to see before being buried in unmarked graves. Placed on their backs, their faces were chalky gray as gravity pulled their blood downward. Turned over they were purplish black. Even counting was sometimes difficult. Bombs and artillery could leave little to count. Did those legs belong to one man or two? Perhaps this arm went with that torso? The dead on our side were whisked away as soon as possible in an attempt that I not see them and report. Later I would suspect that some of the dead Viet Cong were Vietnamese soldiers stripped down to be counted as enemy. For me they eventually came to be objects and not people. I came and counted, made my report and tried to forget. I did it for five years and today I still try not to remember it.

On a far different level, I made an equally uncomfortable discovery: war can be an unparalleled adventure and, for lack of a better word, fun. In a strange way it can provide a new freedom. In this war, we were all separated from people we knew and in a situation where those persons back home would never know what we did. In a war it is easy to believe that the standards of conduct we have followed all our lives no longer apply. Suddenly faced with available helicopters, platoons of protective guards and little accountability, there were things to be hidden and experiences to be had.

I began to see the reporting problem. I think almost all of the U.S. military people on the ground reported as honestly as they could. A glance at any newspaper showed that somewhere between the man on the ground and the published reports, the Pentagon must have favored the numbers from the South over the reports from their own people. By the time of the U.S. military withdrawal, I think every Viet Cong had been killed at least three times.

During the 6 weeks I spent with the District, it was quite safe to walk through the nearby village, buy food and talk with people during the day. This wasn't very smart because the District Chief instantly heard that I spoke Vietnamese. At night it was unsafe to go out of the fortress. Daytime attacks were very rare although they did happen.

I volunteered to drive our open Jeep and trailer into the capitol, Ca Mau, to pick up a barrel of fuel for the generator, drive of about 15 miles each way. On the way back, a grenade was fired at me but it landed in the canal next to the road and sprayed me with water. I arrived back at the District shaken and wet. I'm not sure all of the wetness was water.

The nighttime attacks continued every three or four days. The frustration of our little Advisory Team was evident. Each night, the Vietnamese troops hunkered down and waited to be attacked. During the day, they had nobody to target in return. Patrols at night rarely lead to anything as the Viet Cong melted away back to their homes.

The Phoenix Program was a covert intelligence operation and assassination program undertaken by the US in close collaboration with South Vietnamese intelligence. The program was designed to identify and "neutralize"—capture; induce to surrender; kill; or otherwise disrupt—the combatant and noncombatant infrastructure of Viet Cong cadres who were engaged both in recruiting and training insurgents within South Vietnamese villages, as well as providing support to the North Vietnamese war effort.

The Viet Cong laid down caches of food and equipment for the troops coming from border sanctuaries; it provided guides and intelligence for the North Vietnamese strangers; it conscripted non-volunteer personnel to serve in local force (militia) and main force mobile combat units of the Viet Cong, levied taxes to facilitate the administration of a rudimentary civil government, and enforced its will through terror. In areas more or less loyal to the Saigon government, protection against the North Vietnamese forces—or even VC guerrillas—was often compromised, because an elected village chief would be assassinated, a bomb would explode in the market place, or a Southern patriot would be shot in the back.

Phoenix was a program which resulted in both a refugee problem and greater discontent among the population. The Phoenix program was dangerous, for it was being used against political opponents of the regime, whether they were Viet Cong or not. Phoenix also contributed substantially to corruption. Some local officials demanded payoffs with threats of arrests under the Phoenix program, or released genuine Viet Cong for cash. Some military experts surmised that Phoenix was helping the Viet Cong more than hurting it. By throwing people in prison who were often only low-level operatives — sometimes people forced to cooperate with the VC when they lived in Viet Cong territory — the government was alienating a large slice of the population.

"I never knew in the course of all those operations any detainee to live through his interrogation. They all died. There was never any reasonable establishment of the fact that any one of those individuals was, in fact, cooperating with the VC, but they all died and the majority were either tortured to death or things like thrown out of helicopters."..."It [Phoenix] became a sterile depersonalized murder program... Equal to Nazi atrocities, the horrors of "Phoenix" must be studied to be believed."

(Former "Phoenix" officer Bart Osborne, testifying before Congress in 1971)

One of our team members was the Advisor to the Phoenix Program. "Viet Cong" captured arrived in the middle of the night and were 'interrogated' on the far side of the compound in the absence of the American advisor. I could sometimes hear them scream.

With sufficient torture any person will tell his interrogator anything he wants to hear, just to stop the pain. New leads came from these 'interrogations.' Undoubtedly some of these leads were accurate but some of them must have been an effort to stop the interrogation.

When I questioned the program both the Americans and Vietnamese involved, all older and more experienced than I, swore that the program was carefully run and effective. Today I am ashamed to say that for too long I believed them. A program approved by our President, nothing I could say or do would affect its activities.

I wrote no reports during this six week introduction. I did watch and learn. I learned several things that I thought had little or no solution.

First, almost all information received and reported by the U.S. military came through the Vietnamese. Many American advisors had their own personal interpreters – Vietnamese assigned to them fulltime for this purpose. Without exception, they believed that 'their' interpreter was absolutely honest and totally pro-American. Bullshit!! These men had to live and exist in Viet-Nam and their future and fortunes depended upon the South Vietnamese government. Advisors would come and go but the interpreters would remain. I sometimes heard these interpreters give completely different translations of answers. These mistranslations always made the Vietnamese look better and the Viet Cong look worse. As a result I believe that about 90% of U.S. military reporting reflected exactly what the Vietnamese wished.

Second, the enemy was difficult and often impossible to identify. The Vietnamese and Americans usually could only react.

Third, the Viet Cong were careful to only attack American and Vietnamese troops and installations. With B-52s and artillery, the Americans and Vietnamese caused casualties in the general population. Anger over the deaths of 'neutral' people and reactions to programs like Phoenix meant that the Viet Cong had little trouble recruiting replacements. The Vietnamese, except for a segment of its officer corps, had to draft and coerce replacements.

I thought our small Advisory Team handled the stress well until late one night as we all slept. Suddenly our Medic screamed, *"Oh God, they're in here!!"* Convinced that we had been infiltrated, we all jumped out of bed, bumping into each other and fighting to get into the bunker. The Medic had awoken to find a mouse trapped in his mosquito net. Funny now but not at the time. At least we didn't start shooting at each other in the dark.

Before I left the District I had come to the conclusion that, as long as the U.S. continued to pour in massive amounts of money, materials and troops, the Vietnamese would not lose. They also would never win.

At the end of the six weeks, I packed up and moved into Ca Mau, the capitol city of An Xuyen.

The Advisory Team wasn't small. The Province Senior Advisor (PSA) was an Army colonel; I was the Deputy. In Viet-Nam's 44 provinces, each with an Advisory Team, half were headed by an Army colonel and half by a senior CORDS civilian. At age 26 it would have been absurd to place me in charge and I frankly thought it strange to even be the number two. The team had about 200 Army personnel, mostly support, and an equal number of Vietnamese civilian employees. These civilians worked directly under me. Most of them were drivers, electricians, plumbers, janitors and the like. I had a small staff of about 30 that worked with me to collect information for my reports.

The PSA in Ca Mau, when I moved, stayed only for about a week and rotated home at the end of his tour. I don't even recall his name. He was replaced by Col. John P. King, a tall, bald, non-drinking, non-smoking Southerner. Col. King had been carefully briefed on my role in the province and, thank God, had no problem with it. About 90% of the rest of the Team did have a

problem with it. John stayed as PSA for 3 years and I could not have asked for a better person. We became good friends professionally and personally.

However, John's first staff meeting was not helpful. After introducing himself, he began questioning. *"Who handles local civil government?"* I raised my hand. *"Who handles the hospital?"* I raised my hand. *"Who deals with schools?"* I raised my hand. *"Local militia?"* I raised my hand. *"Roads? Power? Water?"* I raised my hand. *"Gentlemen, I know what HE does. What the hell do the rest of you do?"* What a great way to make me even less popular than I already was!

It soon came back to me that John met with the entire military staff and let them know that any problem I had with any military person would become a real problem that they would have with him. I could not ask for better.

John's Vietnamese counterpart was the Province Chief, a military man who acted as governor of the province, controlling both military and civilian government activities. We went through several Province Chiefs while I was in Ca Mau. They all were corrupt, grasping and greedy men. The position was usually purchased and the incumbent needed to steal as much as possible to pay off the debt incurred. That is not to say that they lacked talent.

History lesson

In 1954, when the French pulled out and Viet-Nam divided, a large number of North Vietnamese left and went south. Over time they became very influential in the South Vietnamese government. After President Kennedy approved the assassination of President Diem, the military took over. From that point on, the President of Viet-Nam would always be a military man. Elections were always fairly honest; the people had a choice of one carefully selected military man or another. The voters picked their President; the military picked the candidates. (end)

Many Province Chiefs were northerners, including several in Ca Mau. One had a northern accent so thick that the population barely understood him in his speeches. These northerners in the military had more of an interest in winning the war than even the southerners. They understood that they would be seen as traitors if the North won the war. They pushed their troops to fight hard but saw no reason this should interfere with their corruption. In Ca Mau, one general forced his wounded to pay for blood and medical treatment. The Province Chief skimmed money off the top of salaries, project funds and operating expenses.

Eventually I quit reporting examples of corruption. There probably were not a sufficient number of qualified and talented honest people to operate the government. Nixon knew the situation. He could, and did, require the Vietnamese to remove those with 'over the top' corruption but the level kept moving upwards until nothing seemed adequate to cause removal. If they could produce results, they could steal as much as possible.

I worked with many fine, honest Vietnamese officers but it appeared to me that, in general, promotions up to the rank of Captain came from merit; above that rank came from corruption and payoffs. (end)

I was there to report on the conduct of the war, the operations of the Vietnamese government and the mood of the population. I used my Vietnamese staff to gather information about government operations, instructing them to develop relationships with the heads of the various departments but also with the lower level staff. As long as they did not inquire about finances, they were able to collect good and accurate information. John, as PSA, worked with the Province Chief and collected information from him but I used my own contacts to confirm information. I had a fine Vietnamese staff and considered some of them good personal friends but I never lost

 sight of the fact that their loyalty was tempered by the need to survive first in the culture they lived in.

I spent a lot of time developing personal relationships with mid-level Vietnamese army and civilian personnel. Thanks to my language ability, I could do this in informal ways, meeting at restaurants or in their homes. Most did not want to be seen entering my compound, knowing that it would be reported to the Province Chief. I also made friends with shopkeepers and others not connected with the Vietnamese government. With my language ability I soon had a good network of people that supplied a wealth of information for my reporting. I made two rules for myself. First, never ask too many questions – usually people would end up volunteering information if they felt that I wasn't using it. Second, make sure that nothing ever was used in such a way that the source could be identified.

The Province Chief assigned me a bodyguard. Sgt. Minh was about 4' 10" and spoke excellent English, perfect for ease dropping on Americans. The Province Chief was 'concerned about my security' but Minh's primary function was to report to the Province Chief all of my meetings and activities. Minh actually was a good guy caught in a terrible position. If he became too much of a problem for me, I would send him back to the Province Chief and his head would roll. We eventually worked it out. After I got to know him, I sat him down and told him that we needed to work out some arrangement. It was a risk but I don't believe that he reported this back to the Province chief.

If I went to a restaurant, I always ate on the second floor for security reasons. The downstairs areas were always open to the street. As a 'bodyguard,' I stationed Minh at the bottom of the stairs. He could honestly say that he did not see me meet anybody and I "probably ate alone." I made a point of asking the person I would meet to arrive first at the restaurant. Naturally a lot of other people saw me meet people in these very public places but without prior knowledge it was not likely that the Province chief could have placed other easedroppers nearby. At meetings in other places he could report that the door where he was stationed was too far away to hear anything. Obviously he had to produce something for the Province Chief once in awhile so I would arrange totally social meetings and even invite him to sit with us. Naturally he then had loads of useless stuff to report back. To the day I left Ca Mau, Minh was at the door when I left in the morning and at the door when I went home. When I left the country on vacation he actually followed me to the ramp of the airplane. He would be there when I returned. He had no personal life.

I began to make reports. One standard report was the Hamlet Evaluation System (HES), designed by the Rand Corporation for Secretary of Defense Robert MacNamara. This report had a variety of questions about each hamlet, village, district and province in Viet-Nam. Crunched through a computer, it produced a grade for each area from A to F, just like school grades. The results were shared with the Saigon government and became a report card on the abilities of the Province Chiefs. At first I shared my input to the report with the Vietnamese. This usually ended up in long arguments.

Questions like "Did the enemy operate in this village during the last month?" should have been simple. For example, the Vietnamese would say no Viet Cong operated there during the month. I would say the village was hit by mortars several times. The Vietnamese would not disagree, but would say, *"Yes, but they were fired from outside the village."* Apparently this meant that the enemy did not operate in the village. I just quit sharing my input. In the end, these reports meant little. We were committed to this war and the powers that made the decisions were trapped into a situation where the truth would not change events.

I wrote a lot of 'think pieces.' The subjects were anything I thought useful and interesting. They seemed to be appreciated and I was encouraged to keep writing them. I thought that having my reports go directly to the basement of the White

House was great until a friend pointed out *"That's also where they keep the incinerator!"*

Many of these reports were on the mood of the population in An Xuyen. I felt that about 80% of the population gave little support to either the Vietnamese or the Viet Cong. They wanted to go on with their life, raise their children and crops and be left alone.

We had one other U.S. organization in Ca Mau – the CIA. I thought they were a disaster. Staffed by two young Americans with no prior experience (Listen to me!), they spoke no Vietnamese and had to depend entirely upon interpreters to collect and relay information. I thought both of them had seen too many James Bond movies. I offered to share information. To them this meant I would give them all of my information and they would give me none. I refused.

After a few months, the CIA withdrew their Americans and left the office operated solely by local Vietnamese. Every few weeks an American CIA person would drive into town, enter their compound and stay hidden for a day or two. They never arrived by air – too noticeable – and were convinced that their movements went undetected. The Team didn't care, frankly. One day I was meeting with a Vietnamese friend who announced, *"I see the CIA is in town."*

"How do you know?"

"Oh, they all drive blue Toyotas." And they did!

Eventually I would receive requests for opinions on things that could have only come from CIA reports. I often thought the information and conclusions were nonsense and said so, careful to back up my opinions with facts. The Ca Mau CIA group went from cold to downright hostile. I quit asking to meet with them.

I had a contact in the Vietnamese Fisheries Office in Ca Mau. I knew that the CIA staff sometimes contacted him. We met one evening for a beer and well, the Devil made me do it. Lying outrageously, I told him I had met a fisherman who had a story about seeing a large piece of equipment being unloaded in an uninhabited area. I went on to describe a large Soviet radar system. Sure enough, a month or so later, I was asked if I could corroborate a CIA report that the Viet Cong had installed a radar system in that same area. I responded that the area was pure mud, had no roads or cover and that a radar unit also needed a large generator. If present it all would have sunk into the mud by now, probably in full view. Still, if it was present it had no discernable use.

The faces of the visiting American CIA people changed but I wanted little to do with them. The feeling was mutual. The Province Chief assigned Capt. Le to be my direct contact for routine business. Le and I became good friends. He was honest, which meant poor. He proved to be a valuable contact that, over time, grew to trust me because I was very careful to see that nothing negative could be traced back to him. A major portion of his job was to get money for various activities. The Province Chief was never going to come with his hand out. At the province level virtually all money for civil government operations except salaries came from the United States – me. I spent many evenings at Le's small house with his children gathered around. His wife, by custom, always remained in the kitchen.

I had in my office a four drawer safe the size of a standard filing cabinet. It was full of Vietnamese currency. When I ran low a radio call to Can Tho would bring a plane down with brown paper grocery sacks full of more money. I accounted for the expenditures but did not need receipts. It was degrading for the Vietnamese to come to the Americans for any funds need to build, repair, equip or train. The system came about because the U.S. recognized that turning money over directly to the Province Chief or any higher level meant that most of it would disappear. Capt. Le would bring proposals to our office and the two of us would discuss them. To the extent feasible, I tried to provide as much as possible to projects in the form of material rather than cash. This dependence upon the Americans for almost everything was embarrassing for all but I saw no better solution. I did make one face saving change.

In the past, requests for funds came directly to my office. I insisted that all requests for money be made to the Province Chief. Approvals or disapprovals then appeared to come from the Province Chief instead of the Americans. Approved activities then worked through Capt. Le.

I had one serious assassination attempt. A man came to my office and asked for a meeting. The armed guard at the office door thought something was strange and ordered him against the wall. In his boot top was a small, single round, home-made 45 cal. pipe pistol cocked and ready to fire. I turned him over to the Phoenix people.

One of the perks in Vietnam was a two week R&R trip every 90 days. Transportation was provided to Bangkok, Manila, Sydney, Australia or Taipei, Taiwan. I took full advantage of them and visited all these places repeatedly. In addition, American Ambassador Ellsworth Bunker was married to another Ambassador, Carol Lasey, posted in Nepal. Bunker was an old retired man who did not want the job but took it as a favor to President Kennedy. Kennedy, in return, provided him with a former Air Force One plane. Every few weeks the plane carried one Ambassador to visit the other. For a few dollars for lunch, I could board the plane to visit Nepal. The Ambassador stayed in the Presidential apartments on the plane while a few of us occupied the former press section. I did this several times.

The days turned into weeks, the weeks into months. I

developed a routine of collecting information, counting casualties, writing reports and dealing with project requests. In December, 1971, I was asked to take another two year contract.

Over time in An Xuyen security slowly improved as the Vietnamese moved outward and the people moved closer to the city. I could now visit places in about half the province. Some villages could even be visited by boat although the Province Chief insisted that a platoon of soldiers accompany me. No resistance on my part. Under the Geneva Convention, signed by the United States, any person 'impersonating' a soldier was a war criminal. I was extremely nervous on these boat excursions with a platoon of soldiers surrounding me. For a Viet Cong hidden on the river bank, faced with a boatload of soldiers and one civilian and one good shot, the natural assumption is that the civilian is the most important person. I felt very vulnerable. The sensible solution was to wear an Army uniform on these trips (No general's stars, however. Actually no insignia at all.) To comply with the Geneva Convention, Col. King decided to list me as a soldier if the need arose – a nice way of saying 'if I was captured'. I assumed that this was all that he did. I should have known that this man, who was strict in doing things right, perhaps did more. He actually did send forward papers through Army channels – and forgot to tell me. Thirty-five years later I received a certificate from the Secretary of the Army and the Chief of Staff for my service in the US Army. No pension attached, unfortunately.

Then there were several other serious assassination attempts. One Viet Cong was captured with a map of my house and my bed location marked. Still yet another was intercepted at the door of my office with another small pipe gun loaded and cocked.

Around this time, the Viet Cong changed tactics in one of the few mistakes I thought they made. In the past they had usually been careful to not cause civilian casualties. They now began terrorist-like activities – bombs placed in the market, for example. The worst incident was the bombing of the only bridge across the river in the center of town. It connected the central city with the only road. It was a reasonable target – the way they did it was not. The Viet Cong constructed a large bomb to float under the surface of the water. By using a rope of the correct length, they could allow the current to carry it under the bridge and stop. It was hand detonated by wire. The bomber could have chosen to blow up the bridge at any time but waited until it was crowded with children going to school. Twenty-three children were killed. A mangled bicycle landed a block away. In a war for the hearts and minds of people, it was a disaster.

Each week I had an Air America helicopter or Army Huey for a day. I used it to visit all over the province and develop relationships with village and hamlet chiefs. It began to look as if the Viet Cong might be pushed into marginal areas of no consequence. The rest of the country did not fare so well. Then President Nixon began the peace talks with North Viet-Nam. Apparently no adults were available so the first six months were spent in arguments over the shape of the table to be used by the negotiators.

After larger firefights with the Viet Cong, I visited the Ca Mau hospital to count wounded. I hated this. Counting the dead is unpleasant but the victims no longer suffer. The wounded were a different matter. The Vietnamese doctors were skilled but overworked. In too many cases a wound to the knee or elbow resulted in amputation because it moved the patient out faster. I always was astonished at the calm attitude of the Vietnamese wounded soldiers.

The hospital, like almost everything else, ran on U.S. funds. A U.S. Army doctor came down to examine the hospital and stayed with me. (There were no hotels in town.) Over dinner I commented on this strange calm attitude of the wounded. The doctor claimed that the major cause of death among American troops was not the wound. It was shock. Seeing themselves wounded, their blood pressure dropped and this often caused death from wounds that were not life threatening. He claimed the Vietnamese are much more fatalistic. If it is time to die, no medical treatment will change the outcome. If it is not the time to die, no lack of medical treatment will change the outcome. It seemed to make sense.

On one visit to the hospital I saw this attitude in action. Sitting on the dirty floor was a boy, about 11 years old, with bloody rags wrapped around his feet. *"What happened?"* I asked.

"My brother is a soldier. He is visiting home and his rifle was lying on the floor. My little sister pulled the trigger and shot me through both ankles."

The boy was calmly waiting for a doctor's attention. No tears or anxiety.

"Doesn't that hurt?"

"Yes," was all that he said. Apparently this fatalistic attitude starts young.

The peace negotiations began and continued endlessly in Paris. President Truman once said, *"The United States has never lost a war or won a conference."* Nixon wanted out of an unpopular and unwinable war and the North Vietnamese knew this.

The province was allocated 6,000 artillery rounds a month for the purpose of Harassment and Interdiction (H&I) fire. Each night, the artillery crews would pick random targets along known pathways of Viet Cong movement and simply fire at them – 200 rounds a night. All the artillery in the province was located around the city since the Province Chief sensibly decided not to run the risk of losing one to the enemy and having it turned toward the city. I thought this program was expensive (It was) and ineffective. I was wrong – captured Viet Cong admitted that the program terrified them. It is possible to go to sleep with the windows rattling and the walls shaking. I could sleep through this roar but would be instantly awake at the sound of small arms fire. Small arms fire meant that there was a ground attack on the city. If this sound came close, I headed for the bunker. One morning I arose to find a bullet that had penetrated the walls of the house, hit the headboard of my bed and half emerged inches from my pillow. I don't know if it hit while I was in bed or in the bunker and didn't care. That day I had bricks stacked around the three sides of my bedroom.

Parallel to the negotiations, Nixon decided on a program of "Vietnamization," declaring that the Vietnamese were now capable of fighting the war with less U.S. presence. In An Xuyen we never had significant numbers of U.S. combat troops so Nixon was correct at least in this area. U.S. troops began to leave the country and the Vietnamese held their ground, albeit with massive U.S. material support.

The final agreement called for a halt to fighting with both sides keeping control of whatever areas they had. A four nation international peace-keeping commission would oversee the ceasefire. In 1973 Col. King and the entire military part of the Advisory Team went to the airport and flew off, leaving, well, me. I was now the Province Senior Advisor with a much reduced Vietnamese staff and no Americans. I returned to our compound to find the Province Chief personally directing the looting of the military part of our compound. Within 48 hours every piece of equipment, windows, doors, wiring and finally lumber stripped out to leave only the concrete foundations of the buildings. Only my office building and the compound where I lived – with three other now empty houses – were untouched.

With the departure of the US military, CORDS began to change. The Corps Commanders, like John Vann, were replaced by the State Department and Consulate Generals. The first Consul General in Can Tho was Wolfgang Lehmann, a naturalized American from Germany. Lehmann was a career diplomat who had spent most of his career in Europe. He arrived and tried to establish a more traditional Consulate. He called in his new staff of CORDS people. I think he was expecting a group of diffident young career Ivy League FSOs. What he got was a group of battle hardened individuals with years of experience disagreeing with State, the military, the CIA and sometimes each other. He didn't seem to quite know what to do with us.

Shortly after his arrival, each province received a new diffident young Ivy League FSO. Mine was a guy named Madden. He spoke no Vietnamese and had no experience in the country. He spent hours with the Province Chief and a few ranking officials in the province and began to write a long report. When he showed me his draft, I began to point out factual errors and wrong conclusions based upon them. This made him coldly furious and he stopped showing me his work. Once again the White House began to get reports from CORDS and State that disagreed. After about five weeks, all these FSOs were withdrawn and posted elsewhere. I went on as usual sending the usual reports and writing on any subject of interest. Lehmann didn't seem to know what to do with us and we saw little of him after the State Department FSOs left.

In a few days after the US military left the peace-keeping commission arrived. It originally had the Canadians, Iranians (still under the Shah), Poles and Hungarians. The Canadians and Iranians took over two of the empty houses on my compound. The Communist Poles and Hungarians moved into an old French villa supplied by the Province Chief. It soon bristled with antennas.

In spite of the ceasefire and 'stay in place' agreement both sides moved to grab as much land area as possible. I still had Air America helicopters available but it was impossible to monitor all this activity. I could not trust the Vietnamese now to accurately report their actions. There was no real ceasefire and both sides claimed all actions were initiated by the other side.

After a few months, the Canadians recognized the futility of participating and withdrew. They were replaced by the Indonesians. When they arrived, I received a message from the Embassy in Saigon that a plane would pick me up that afternoon. Somehow the Embassy knew that I spoke both Vietnamese and Indonesian. I was asked to translate between the Vietnamese and Indonesians at a cocktail party at the Ambassador's Residence. Neither language was a problem but I had never attempted to translate directly from one to the other. I left with a horrible headache. Tibor Nagy, a naturalized American from Hungary had a great time. He cornered the Hungarians and regaled them (in Hungarian) with his stories of deserting from the Hungarian Army, crawling under the border barbed wire with his infant son during the unsuccessful Hungarian revolution in 1955 and immigrating to the United States where he now earned more money each month than the entire Hungarian delegation. The Hungarians sat stone faced as Tibor laughed and carried on. Hardly diplomatic but nobody else could understand the conversation.

The fighting went on with no major changes in controlled area. For those of us still in the country, it became clear that Nixon and the U.S. would not continue to supply the Vietnamese at former levels in spite of claiming to do so. The artillery rounds supplied to the province dwindled down to about 200 a month. The Province Chief was afraid to use even these in case the city was attacked. Soldiers in the outposts in the countryside could no longer call for artillery support when attacked.

The average time for an American soldier to be med-evaced after being wounded was four minutes. The med-evacs picked up all wounded, both American and Vietnamese. With the departure of U.S. troops the soldiers now depended upon the Vietnamese for med-evacs. I began to get stories of wounded soldiers being asked for money before being evacuated, of the wounded needing to pay for blood transfusions at the hospital. The willingness of the Vietnamese troops to take risks dropped quickly. They began to lose control.

The Vietnamese held on through 1973 and most of 1974 but the end was in sight. In my opinion Nixon wanted enough time to pass after our departure before the country collapsed so that he could claim the Vietnamese lost – not the U.S.

I spent most of my time now writing 'mood of the people' reports. It appeared to me that, in An Xuyen at least, most of the people did not want the Viet Cong to win and did not want to live under a Communist system. But they were beginning to realize that the war, already underway for 30 years, could continue for many more years. They were tired of it. They mostly did not change sides as much as slowly stop supporting the Vietnamese government. Army desertions increased as troops left to go home. By November, 1974, I was Province Senior Advisor to three provinces that covered about 20% of the entire country as the U.S. presence continued to decline. I traveled from one to the other each day by helicopter.

In December, 1974, those of us left in the IV Corps CORDS program withdrew to Can Tho, the Corps headquarters. The

Consul General Lehmann was replaced by the State Department with Terry MacNamara.

I was sitting at my desk when a short rotund guy with a blue and white striped shirt and Italian boots with three inch heels plopped down in front of me.

"You Kassebaum?"

"Yes."

"I understand you speak good Vietnamese."

"Yes."

"This evening I want you to take me on a tour of all the local whore houses!"

"Who the hell are you?"

"Terry MacNamara, the new Consul Genreal."

"Yes, sir!"

I had no idea what this was about and didn't like the idea at all. At about 7 in the evening the Consul General's chauffeured car rolled up to my door. The American Flag flew on the fenders lit up with small lights.

There were dozens of bars/whore houses in Can Tho. There were 5 or 6 within a block of the Consulate. I gave the driver directions to one of them.

I was sweating furiously as the clearly marked car stopped directly at the door. MacNamara hauled me into the smoky crowded place.

"Tell the girl I want to see the owner," said MacNamara.

"Oh, God," I thought. *"Maybe he wants group rates."* The owner, always an older women in these places, arrived.

"Tell her who I am." (And I thought this couldn't get worse!) I introduced him. Through me they exchanged pleasantries – both professionals at that I thought.

"Tell her that if she has any problem with any American for any reason, I want her to come see me personally. Don't go to the police or the Province Chief – come see me first. I guarantee that she will be shown into my office and we will take care of the problem."

What a relief! After a few more pleasantries, we departed for the next place. We repeated this long into the night. Naturally word of this reached every American in IV Corps and, you know, there never was a problem.

Well, almost never. Three or four of us went to lunch at "Nancy's Fancy Juices," a bar/restaurant/whore house across the street from the Consulate. It was open to the street, brightly lit by the sun in the front and quite dark at the back. As we sat having lunch, an American who shall remain nameless entered and went to the bar. He did not see us in the darkness. He collared the waitress at the bar.

"I want all the girls out here right now!" he demanded. Soon a group of half clad and half awake girls gathered around him.

"I just came from the doctor and I have the clap. I got it from YOU...... or YOU......or YOU...... or YOU!" he practically shouted.

He saw us when we started laughing and hooting. Red faced, he fled. Over the next 25 years our paths would occasionally cross and he always avoided me for some reason.

MacNamara appointed Hank Cushing as his deputy. Hank was a tall gaunt former professor of English from Notre Dame University. He quoted Dante and Shakespeare, had little patience and a rapier devastating wit for those who displeased him. I found him quite intimidating. He had been in Viet-Nam for more than ten years but didn't speak three words of Vietnamese yet wrote highly intelligent accurate reports. Just my luck – he liked me.

One weekend Hank announced that he had found a really interesting restaurant in a town about 20 miles away. He wished to eat there and I would go with him. We took a Consulate car and went for lunch.

The restaurant sat on a canal and the specialty was turtle. We ordered one. It arrived boiled and on its back. With a flourish, the young waiter pulled off the bottom of the shell to reveal the innards. He headed off but I called him back. *"Hey, you need to show me what to eat and what to not eat."* With a pleasant laugh, he picked up some chopsticks, rummaged around the inside of the turtle and threw a lot of stuff into the canal. *"There! The rest is very good."* And it was. Hank and I spent several hours eating lunch. The place wasn't crowded, the setting was pleasant and so we stayed on and had dinner there also.

There was a curfew after dark. In Can Tho American vehicles were allowed out after curfew. We stayed much too late and now needed to drive the 20 miles back to Can Tho after dark. The road crossed 5 or 6 canals. At curfew, rolls of barbed wire were strung across the road and the bridges guarded by a platoon of soldiers. Hank had spent the afternoon drinking beer and was not feeling much pain but still drove. He pulled up to the wire across the road at the first canal and stopped. A very young red-faced soldier, clearly half drunk, staggered over to the car with his M-16 rifle. Before he could say anything Hank barked, *"Tell this little shit to get that rifle out of my face and move the damned wire!"* Hank's words were not understood but the tone certainly was.

"The bridge is closed and you cannot cross." The barrel of the rifle began to look very large. Hank looked even more annoyed and began to say something. To my own surprise, I said, *"Hank,*

SHUT UP – not one word! Let me take care of this." Hank, my intimidating boss, looked astonished but he did stop talking. I asked the soldier to come around to my side of the car. I explained who we were and that we need to get back to Can Tho. I told him I was glad he took his job so seriously and that he was doing the right thing but obviously we were not Viet Cong. I handed him a few banknotes. He smiled and moved the wire. We drove on.

As we approached the next canal I told Hank again to stay silent. He looked like he was going to explode but he did stay quiet. I talked our way through. After that the other bridge guards assumed we were OK because we had crossed the previous canals. At each of these we had no problem.

A week or so later Hank called me into his office to tell me that he had changed my A.I.D. job category from Rural Development Officer to Program Officer. This meant absolutely nothing to me since I didn't know what a Rural Development Officer did, much less a Program Officer, since I had never worked for A.I.D. This seemingly unimportant change saved my career later.

South Viet-Nam was in its death throes. We placed bets on when the country would collapse. Even the most pessimistic of us missed by 6 months. None of us expected the country to collapse as fast at it did.

I still believe the North Vietnamese did not win the war; the

South Vietnamese just gave up. Under no real pressure, the Vietnamese along the northern border began to retreat. It turned into a route. Thousands, then tens of thousands of soldier and civilians started to flee southward. Years later General Giap, head of the North Vietnamese army, would claim that this retreat was so unexpected that he feared a trap and held his army back from pursuing the fleeing troops.

Ships were dispatched to the northern ports of Hue and Danang to pick up people. President Thieu feared that the presence of these refugees would trigger further panic and ordered them taken to Phu Quoc Island, near the Cambodian border to keep them away from rest of the population. U.S. Merchant Marine ships in the area joined in the effort. Within days over 50,000 people were headed for Phu Quoc Island.

In previous years the Vietnamese government had operated a huge prison on Phu Quoc for captured Viet Cong. It had been closed for some years but the rows of barracks remained. MacNamara sent me to the island to monitor the situation and do what I could to assist.

Air America carried me out to the island where I moved into a small trailer on the Vietnamese Navy Base. I took one staff member with me along with a radio. By the time I arrived a few ships had unloaded their cargo of refugees. The camp was some miles from the harbor and transportation difficult to find. The next day a cargo plane brought me a Jeep.

The camp provided shelter but little else. The system of five wells that supplied water no longer worked. I used the radio to talk with Bill Binns, the CORDS person in Rach Gia, the closest mainland town. The U.S., Australia and Taiwan began to fly in planes full of rice and other food. The refugees had no way to cook the rice – a serious and immediate problem. Ships were beginning to pile up just outside the port, bringing more and more refugees. The Navy Base had a few tanker trucks that carried water to the camp but the supply was inadequate. Unless the refugees had food and water, there was the possibility that they might invade the small town around the Navy Base and riot. I asked Binns if he could send water pumps and cooking pots as soon as possible. He signed off saying, *"I'll do something."*

The next morning I stood on the beach and saw a large barge from Rach Gia being towed into the harbor. In the center of the barge was a large shiny red fire truck with "Rach Gia" painted on the side. Stacked around it were thousands of steel Army helmets. Bill had solved both problems with ingenuity! The fire truck pumped water from the wells and the steel Army helmets made excellent cooking pots.

Serious problems were developing on some of the ships anchored in the harbor. Along with the civilian refugees the ships had numerous army deserters. They were armed and often dangerous. Some robbed and raped. The ship's crews wanted them unloaded as soon as possible. The Vietnamese Navy feared that these armed deserters could take over the refugee camp and perhaps even the town. The Navy agreed to unload the ships only by landing craft. These are small landing craft designed to carry troops and equipment from ship to beach. Each could only carry about 200 people tightly packed. The ship captains wanted to dock and unload quickly.

The worst situation was on a U.S. Merchant Marine ship, the Pioneer Contender. The crew was split between the wheelhouse and the engine room, locked behind the steel bulkheads. About a thousand refugees had the rest of the ship along with a group of deserters. The deserters were robbing and terrorizing the refugees and firing their weapons at the crew if they tried to interfere. By radio the desperate captain of the ship told me that he would dock with or without permission. The Navy told me that they would sink his ship if he attempted to enter the harbor, fearing a much greater problem if the deserters got loose on the island with arms and ammunition. I was caught in the middle. The Navy agreed to unload the Pioneer Contender first but still only by landing craft. The cursing and swearing ship captain had no choice.

The Navy surrounded one dock with barbed wire and mounted 50 cal. machine guns on each side. The wire formed a funnel. As the landing craft brought in the refugees, they were squeezed down to a single file and disarmed at gunpoint. The

Navy Lt. in charge of the dock used a bullhorn and made it clear that any person who resisted would be shot. There was no resistance.

As they passed off the dock, some refugees pointed out deserters and accused them of various serious crimes on the ship. The man accused was hauled to one side into a pen. If the same man was accused a second time by other refugees, he moved to a second pen. After the third accusation, the man was hauled down to the beach a few yards from the dock. Tough and vicious on the ship, they begged and pleaded now. A firing squad executed them; the Lt. finishing the job with a shot to each head from his pistol. (Throughout my years in Viet-Nam I never took pictures of war dead. We had a policy against this type of picture but, more importantly, I saw little reason to want them as souvenirs. For some unexplained reason, in this single incidence, I did photograph the executions. I still don't know why. Perhaps because I knew the war was over.)

It took a few days to unload all the ships. Still cursing at me, the captain of the Pioneer Contender steamed away. I would see this ship again.

After two weeks, the Red Cross and other agencies, along with the Navy, had the camp functioning in a primitive but safe way. Food and medicine supplies were arriving regularly. I flew back to Can Tho. The end was near.

Nixon got his 'decent interval.' Two years after the U.S. military left, the collapse of Vietnamese resistance in the north part of the country had turned into a full scale rout. Gen. Giap's North Vietnamese Army began to move south meeting almost no resistance. At times they could barely keep up with the fleeing Vietnamese troops. Saigon fell on April 29.

I will always maintain that North Viet-Nam did not win the war; the South just quit resisting. I do not know what minor event triggered the collapse of the South. In my opinion, the people of the South never decided that they preferred Communism. They did decide that the war could go on for another 30 years and they were tired of it. Many chose peace under Communism over endless war under a corrupt semi-democracy. The United States escalated the war to incredible violent levels after years of low level insurgency. We equipped and taught the Vietnamese to fight like the U.S. Army and then pulled out and slowed the flow of support.

Almost from the day I arrived in Viet-Nam I thought that neither the South nor the North could ever win. I did believe that they could and would reach an accommodation. After all, in all the long centuries of Viet-Nam's history the country had rarely been united. It was most often two or even three different countries. I thought history gave it a chance to peacefully co-exist with its northern neighbor. I was wrong. In the end, the North Vietnamese had little reason to negotiate. We had underestimated the resolve and capability of Ho Chi Minh's forces and perhaps had even forgotten our own American revolution. George Washington had understood that when fighting a much larger, better equipped and organized enemy, the way to success is not winning battles or holding territory, but to simply keep fighting. Eventually your foe will decide that the war is no longer worth the cost. Washington only won two significant battles in our revolution but kept up the fighting until the British concluded that it was no longer worth continuing. Invading Vietnam was a mistake but the bigger mistake was not recognizing it sooner.

When the end finally comes on April 29, 1975, our small group of 10 Americans and almost 300 Vietnames employees from the Consulate in the Delta leave in two small landing crafts and a wooden Vietnamese fishing boat. We assembled the employees and families who wish to escape at two compounds. The guards are ordered to see that the only people allowed into the compounds are those leaving with us. We all fear that an obvious departure would trigger anything from a riot to join us to a riot in anger over the final demise of the South Vietnamese government. To our relief, the guards stay loyal to us to the end and control the access to the compounds.

The three small boats are tightly packed with almost 300 Vietnamese by the time we pull away from shore. We have a few unexpected people but overall our departure goes smoothly. Just pulling away from shore is a major relief for us all.[1]

After only an hour or two, we transfer the people from the wooden boat onto the landing crafts. The fishing boat is unable to keep up with the landing craft and is too unstable when towed. This makes the space aboard the landing craft almost standing room only.

Let me step back a few weeks at this point. Jim Tully is one of my neighbors. Jim has been in Vietnam a long time and speaks Vietnamese very well. With the collapse of the country now obvious, Jim and the other married people attached to the Consulate have been ordered to leave.

Jim is a compact man who has a history of exotic wives and children. Marriages don't seem to last for Jim but he makes sure that his various children receive support. In Vietnam Jim married again – this time to a very young Vietnamese girl. Jim and Tuyet have a small son, Kimo, who is about 5 years old.

Jim has hired a Cambodian boy named Bung to look after Kimo. Apparently Jim and Bung have formed an attachment to each other.

1

For details of this phase of the evacuation, see Terry McNamara's "Escape With Honor" or James Butler's "Saigon." Both detail the trip.

A few days before Jim and family are to leave Vietnam, Jim comes to my house. He and his family are leaving the next day and Jim has a request.

Jim Tully wants me to promise to take out Bung, the boy who looks after his five-year-old son. Jim, Tuyet and son Kimo are packed and ready to leave for Saigon to catch the planes out of the country. The evacuation departure planes are closely monitored. American government people, contractors and other married or non-essential personnel are being hustled out of the country, as the fall of South Vietnam becomes more evident every day. There is no way that Tully can convince anybody that 12 year old Cambodian Bung is a member of his family or otherwise qualified for evacuation. (Vietnamese and Cambodians do not look similar.) Frankly, it isn't clear to me why Tully "owed it" to Bung. Jim makes no mention of discussing this plan with Bung's family. Under the circumstances I made it clear to Jim that I would have no involvement in getting Bung out of the country.

With Tully's departure, Bung disappears. I presume he went back to his family in Can Tho because he obviously could not stay in Tully's empty house. Out of sight, I forget about him.

On the landing craft, things have settled down a bit. I looked down into the crowd in our landing craft and see Bung. He favored very loud clothes and clashed in both color and design.

"How did you get here!"

"My mother sent me for bread in the market. When I passed the compound I saw lots of people." All the guards knew Bung. *"I asked my friend on guard to let me in – and he did!"*

"Does your family know you are leaving with us?"

"No," he said glumly, *"They don't know I'm here."*

There is nothing that could be done at this point.

Twelve hours later we finally locate an American ship, the Pioneer Contender. This is the same ship that was under siege at the Phu Quoc Island port and that I had a shouting match with the captain over the radio. The Vietnamese are placed in the empty cargo hold. I ask one Vietnamese family to look after Bung. I don't expect much. Vietnamese and Cambodians had only the barest tolerance of each other after centuries of rivalry over the Delta. Although neighbors in tightly packed cities and villages, they rarely mix. In the stress of the evacuation, where these people are leaving their extended families, their homes, their culture, history, and traditions, and facing an unknown future, I didn't really expect anybody to expend much effort on this lost Cambodian boy. Bung is the only Cambodian aboard.

We leave our Vietnamese friends on the Pioneer Contender but we know they will receive adequate care. Our handful of Americans work our way from ship to ship to arrive at the USS

Blue Ridge, the command ship of the 7th Fleet conducting the evacuation.   Five days later we reach Subic Bay in the Philippines.

Our group disbands after checking in with the Embassy and receiving vouchers for air travel. The Philippine government will not allow the 100,000 Vietnamese refugees to land. The ships are now steaming directly towards American Guam. I am ordered to Guam to help with the emergency care this huge group will need. Duty calls but we are all demoralized and very tired. Consul General McNamara and I end up on the same flight to Guam.

In Guam the US military has already constructed a huge tent city to house, feed and provide medical care to the refugees. As a Vietnamese linguist, I am asked to do triage at dockside to get the arriving refugees heading the right direction.

On the third ship that I meet, our former staff and a lonely and scared Bung comes down the ramp. I simply do not have the time to deal with this. I order (as if that carried any weight at this point) a former employee, Sgt. Minh (not the bodyguard), to take care of the boy and let me know where he ends up in the tent city.

After a week of this, I am ordered to proceed to Fort Chaffee, Arkansas, to work in the newly established refugee camp. Chaffee has been closed since the early 50's.   The Army reopened it from the mothball stage. It is now fully functioning and ready to receive its new tenants.

Like most of us from the Delta, I feel an obligation to look after those people who had worked for us. I have promised to assist three families. This is some 18 people, with children, older parents, cousins, and whatnot from the usual large and extended Vietnamese family. I'm concerned that they may be dispersed to the several camps planned in the U.S. McNamara agrees, pulls some strings, and arranges for these families to join a military cargo plane at Guam's Anderson Air Force Base for a direct flight to Fort Chaffee rather than randomly be assigned to any of the other refugee camps in the States. He and I discussed Bung and agree that the boy will undoubtedly fall through some crack where his chances of connecting up with Tully will be minimal. These direct flights are initially for former employees and family only. Bung does not fit any of the categories and faces being left behind alone in Guam. McNamara has a simple solution. As "my" three families are checked and loaded onto the buses for Anderson Air Force Base, he and I load Bung into our rented car and follow.

At the Anderson air base, the officials handling the flight are somewhat awed by Consul General McNamara's rank and let us follow the refugees to the side of the plane for a final "good-bye." I push Bung into the crowd of passengers and tell him to simply get on the plane, sit down, and play dumb. McNamara and I say our good-byes to our former employees and watch the Air Force personnel count heads several times. Each count comes up with one extra passenger. Nobody says a word and, although the crew is suspicious, they are not expecting a child to be the possible "sneak." The pilot is eager to leave. As expected, the crew finally says the hell with it and the plane leaves.

By the end of the week, all the refugees have safely landed in Guam. The military has the situation in hand and does not need a group of tired and mentally strung out civilians fresh from Vietnam on their hands at the same time. I'm sharing a hotel room with McNamara and we both decide that it is time to go move on. The flight is a very long one and requires a night spent in Honolulu.

Terry asked me where I would spend the night in Honolulu. *"Wherever the airline puts me."*

"You can stay with me."

"Where are you staying?"

"With my ex-wife and her husband."

This was too bizarre to miss.

Terry's ex-wife was charming, her husband was missing and several of Terry's five daughters wandered about without saying much.

Home again

I had no regrets at having spent all those years in Vietnam. They had not been pleasant but they were not dull either. It gave me a tremendous story and a vital chunk of history to recount. It deepened my comprehension of war: its brutality, violence, chicanery, repression, hypocrisy, deceit, intolerance, and senselessness. I learned this not from books, but from experience. I had also seen some fulfillment in men's lives, some courage, and fortitude in people, decency and honesty and goodwill towards others.

I had also found that as an American abroad in Asia, no matter how long you worked, you remain a foreigner. No matter how well you spoke the languages, absorbed their culture and knew the people, made friends and immersed yourself in life, you are forever a foreigner.

During the five days it took to arrive in the Philippines I was out of touch with my family. When I finally called they were greatly relieved. Television had covered much of the evacuation and, as usual, apparently concentrated on the worst of it.

In Honolulu I left the next morning for D.C. Our group of CORDS people was assigned to operate the refugee camps set up on empty military bases in Pennsylvania, California, Florida, and

Arkansas. I had asked for Fort Chaffee in Fort Smith, Arkansas because it was only two hours from my family. About 20 days after the collapse of Viet-Nam I finally arrived home. After 48 hours I needed to get to Fort Chaffee as the 50,000 refugees poured into the base.

We divided the Fort into 4 areas. I had about 15,000 Vietnamese and Cambodians to look after. The Arkansas National Guard provided me with a small team with a major, a captain and 10 NCOs. Tom O'Dell from our CORDS group arrived a few days later as my deputy.

Problems developed almost as soon as the first refugees arrived. Used to living in their home villages with large families for support, they now were crowded into barracks mixed with total strangers. The frictions lead to fights. Some had old scores to settle with others who ended up in the same camp. In short order I had about a dozen men locked up in the base jail. I used the P.A. system in the barracks to make sure that everybody knew the results of troublemaking. The problems reduced down to an acceptable level.

Boredom was a major problem. I decided that each barracks should elect a leader; groups of ten barracks leaders selected an area leader. The area leaders selected a camp representative who had a desk in my office. With a semblance of self-government I looked for ways to keep people occupied. I required each area to find teachers and start schools for the children.

Just finding people was a major problem – especially with 30,000 people named 'Nguyen!' I had the leaders develop a system to track down people. The P.A. system did not work very well to find people. They often wandered into the other camps or were in clinics or interviews.

One afternoon a Vietnamese who works on the records comes into my office to announce that a boy wants to meet me. *"He says he knows you."*

"Well, let him in."

Bung walks in looking like he has reached the end of his emotional rope. He looks at his feet and asks; *"You know where Tully is?"*

"No, I don't but I'll find him for you." I haven't looked for Bung. In the current mess, it is far easier for him to find me.

We talk a bit. Bung takes me back to his barracks so that I know where he is. I ask him if he would like to work in my office. He needs something to do to take his mind off his troubles and the uncertainty he faces. We need somebody to find people since there is no telephone system in the barracks. He also speaks Cambodian. We need a Cambodian translator in the office.[2] He is eager to spend time with any familiar face.

Bung shows up each day at the office and proves to be a reliable and hard worker. We often need to speak with a particular refugee. With nothing to do in the camp, that person often is not in their barracks. Bung tracks them down even if he has to wander all over the very large camp to find them.

Finding Tully proves to be much more difficult. Tully's contractor job ended after leaving Vietnam. The State Department has no useful forwarding address and his former employer only has a post office box in Honolulu. I cannot find him. Each day Bung asks. Each day his face looks darker as he realizes that Tully may not be found. I have too many other things to do and cannot spend much time on the search.

After a week passes, I receive a call from Washington from a friend who has located a relative of Tully in Honolulu. She has Tully's phone number – in Bangkok! I stay late that night at the camp to call him since there is a 12-hour time difference. Bung stays in the office with me. The connection isn't very good.

"Jim, I'm here in the refugee camp in Arkansas and Bung is here also. He wants to talk with you." I hand the phone to Bung. He

---

I have a group of 25 Cambodians who were in Texas learning to fly fighters. They decide that they want to return home after the end of the war. The Red Cross arranges for them to return. The new Communist government of Cambodia met them at the airport and shot them in full view of the Red Cross escorts.

says a few words. Tully is doing most of the talking. Bung's face goes from excited to longer and darker.   Finally, without responding at all to Tully, he hands me the phone.

"Kass, I told him that I would come and take him out of the camp. But he is a kid without his parents, has no passport and the Thais are not about to let another Cambodian into the country after the flood across the border. I can't get away from here for another couple of months. Will he be alright in the camp?"

"Jim, if you wait a couple of months he won't be in the camp. The state of Arkansas is concerned about all these kids here who are 'unaccompanied minors' without family. The legislature has passed a law to place the ones left here in 30 more days into Arkansas orphanages."

There is a long pause. *"Kass, I told him I would take him and I meant it. Can YOU take him out of the camp until I get there?"*

"I've already taken 18 ex-employees and their families. I've dumped them on my parents. I don't think that's going to work."

"So what's one more?"

Well, he has a point. I did not really want to do this but I don't want to see Bung left in some orphanage after all that he has been through.

"You are absolutely sure you'll come and get him?"

"I'll make a trip there in a few weeks and make arrangements somehow."

"OK, but don't delay. The others can take care of themselves but this is different."

"I really appreciate it. Let me explain it to Bung."

I give the phone back to Bung. He listens and his face begins to brighten up. He hands the phone back to me but Tully is gone.

Bung says, *"Tully says I should stay with you until he comes."*

"It's late. You go back to your barracks and I'll see what we can do tomorrow."

When I arrive at the office the next morning Bung is sitting on the steps. While he did his messenger job, I call one of the placement people and set up a meeting during the lunch hour. I explain the problem over the phone and am surprised to find a willingness to work something out. In truth, with over 100,000 refugees to place, the placing agencies were not inclined to turn down any offers.

Bung and I arrive at the placement office to find that the caseworker has retrieved his file. I assume, as a bachelor with an imperiled job and 18 other refugees, that this will be a difficult request. It is not and I have Bung's papers to leave the camp in about 30 minutes. As I talk with the caseworker, I translate for Bung. From Bung's impassive face, I can't tell if he is pleased or not about this turn of events. I think he assumed that he would be able to stay in the camp until Tully came.

While driving back to the office, I could tell that Bung is working this all out. I assure him that things will be fine and that Tully will be arriving soon to pick him up. He becomes more animated and seems to be moving this whole situation into a positive light. By the time we arrive back at the office, he is eager to run back to the barracks and collect his few things. As I park, he throws open the car door and runs toward the barracks. I see him give a little skip as he disappears into the crowds. While he is gone, I ask the staff to keep him busy for the rest of the day.

He is back in a few minutes with a small bag containing everything he owns. I hear him excitedly telling the Vietnamese staff his story. *"I'm leaving the camp today and my friend will come and get me soon!"* The Vietnamese do not meet this with great enthusiasm. As I work during the afternoon, it becomes clear that the Vietnamese feel that this Cambodian boy has received a break that should have gone to one of them – and perhaps they are right. It is subtle but the prejudice between Vietnamese and Cambodians is evident. Poor Bung has faced this for his entire life and it is beginning to piss me off.

When I arrived in Fort Smith, I rented a three-bedroom

apartment in preparation for assisting my ex-employees. The apartment managers gave me a short-term lease but balked at this when they found out my plans. The families that I sponsored are now in Oklahoma City with my parents. The only single person in this group, Sgt. Minh, has one bedroom, I have another, and I decide that Bung will stay with me and take the third bedroom. The reaction of the staff makes me uneasy about sending him to my family where Vietnamese would surround him. He doesn't speak a word of English and would have to depend upon them to translate. Somehow I know this will not work.

After the office closes, Bung and I drive out of the camp. He has to produce his new papers to get past the guards. On the short drive back to the apartment we talk about the future.

"Tully will get me soon!"

"Yes, I'm sure he will. In the meantime, you and I will work things out. Sgt. Minh will be there while I'm at work. You can work on English."

"Why? Tully speaks Vietnamese."

"Bung, nobody here speaks Vietnamese. You will have to learn English." This is met with no enthusiasm at all.

"Tully speaks Vietnamese, Tuyet speaks Vietnamese."

Bung, at age 12, has dealt with more than most kids his age and is single-minded at best. I let it drop.

Back at the apartment I explain the situation to Minh and ask him to look after Bung while I am at work. I do not detect much interest in this. For the rest of the evening and through dinner, Bung's whole conversation centers on Tully and the future.

In the morning at breakfast, I give Bung a note to keep in his pocket if he leaves the apartment. It has my phone number and a short explanation of who Bung is. The town of Fort Smith is paranoid about the possibility of 50,000 crazed Vietnamese running amuck from the camp. I tell him to stay in the apartment area and not stray off. I also tell Minh to make sure that he knows where Bung is if he does go out.

I'm not in my office for more than two hours when the phone rings. The Fort Smith police have picked up Bung. They believe he is some escapee from the camp and that my note is a fake. I assure them that he is legal and has every right to be "out."

That evening we discuss the day. It is clear that Minh is not going to be much help with Bung. I suggest to Bung that he might want to come into work with me each day and continue his work as messenger and translator. His run-in with the local police made him fearful of leaving the apartment. He finds America scarier than he expects. He agrees and that becomes our routine. He rapidly becomes a bit of a celebrity in the camp, holding court and explaining with great authority about "outside" – not that he understands much of it.

As the days became weeks, the relationship between Bung and I does not change greatly. He is with me while he waits for Tully. I look after him to prevent him from placement in an orphanage. We both expect this to be temporary. A week turned into four, then six. I call Tully in Bangkok again.

"So when are you getting here?"

"I'm really tied up. Soon. I need some more time."

"Here – you tell Bung."

Bung's face goes from happy to sad as he listens. Finally he hands the phone back to me.

"OK, I'll be there in a few days," Tully said.

Jim arrives five days later. He takes a cab to the apartment and arrives in the evening. Bung and I sit down with him. I must give Jim credit for honesty. He says it directly to Bung.

"Bung, I can't take you. I can't leave Bangkok now and there is no way you can go there. The government won't let you. And I don't have any friends or relatives that will take you."

Bung simply wilts, lowers his head and says nothing. We switch to English.

"How can you do this? This boy left Vietnam on your promises. He can't go back and he has nobody here. You can't do this to him!"

Jim has nothing to say. He stands, says good-bye to both of us, and leaves. I have no idea where he goes or stays that night – and don't care. Tully wasn't in the apartment more than 15 minutes.

"Bung, this has been a long day, it's late, and we both need to think about this. Let's talk in the morning."

Bung walks back to his room with slumped shoulders but does not show any emotion in front of me. I go to bed angry and upset.

The next morning is Sunday and no work. We have breakfast and Minh disappears. Bung and I talk.

"Bung, there are several things we can do. You can go back to the camp and look for another sponsor – but if you don't get one, you'll be sent to an orphanage. We can try to get you back to Vietnam and your family but I really don't think that can happen for a long, long time. We can look for people you know and see if they can take care of you." I explain about the orphanages. *"Think about it. I'll help you with whatever you decide."*

This is a heavy burden to put on a 12 year-old but I really don't know what else to do. Bung sits quietly for about 15 minutes. I leave him alone.

"Well, what have you decided?" Large tears roll down his cheeks but he does not make a sound.

"I want to stay here."

My heart sinks. This is not an option as far as I am concerned. Yes, I like kids. Still, I am a 31-year old bachelor with no job security, an uncertain future of my own and no real desire to take on this kind of responsibility. I don't know what to say. We sit silently at the small table in the kitchen. Bung and I have never considered this as a permanent arrangement. Neither of us have any particular feelings toward each other in this temporary situation. My lack of a response tells Bung everything. After a few moments he lays his head on the table and cries.

Throughout this entire ordeal, I have not seen Bung cry. Not after leaving his family, his country, being left alone in refugee camps or dumped into a strange country. It all comes crashing down on him.

I really felt trapped at this moment and wished Tully would get sent to hell – and quickly.

"I don't have anybody." Bung says. *"Don't send me back to the camp,"*

Everything in me says, *"Don't do this. You just can't handle this on top of everything else."* Something else says, *"You can't NOT do this."* I really don't know what to do.

"OK, Bung. We'll give it a try."

It is tough at first. Bung did not leave Vietnam to be with me. I have great feelings of dread that I won't be able to deal with this. We both have been making the best of a temporary situation.

For some days, in the evening in the apartment, Bung sits across the room while we watch television or I read. He does not say much. There is a thick air of sadness in the room. In a few days he sits on one end of the sofa while I sit on the other. Soon, he sits next to me. I am very concerned about this entire situation. I looked into placing him in a foster home. Any action to do this will have him first placed into the state system. He could end up anywhere and without my knowledge. It did not seem like a good option. If I stay with the government, how can I deal with another foreign post with a boy who has no legal relationship with me? I am afraid of becoming too attached to this boy. What if we can't work out the legalities? What will this do to both of us if he has to be placed elsewhere?

With each day, Tully becomes more remote for Bung. After all that had happened to this boy, I did not want him hurt again. I contact a lawyer about legal custody in Oklahoma since that is my legal residence. Adoption never entered my mind. Lacking any other person interested in his welfare and no interest on the part of the state of Oklahoma, the custody process is completed with little difficulty. At least I'm able to assure him, *"Nobody will take you away now."*

Progress with Bung is slow. I wasn't his father and never would be. He learns a very little English but develops a group of buddies his own age in the apartment area. He plays tennis and wins a prize for his age group. He swims in the apartment pool. He changes his name after we discuss it. Bung, pronounced "Bum" – a double disadvantage – just isn't going to help him. I try delicately to explain that, unfortunately, his name has to go – or he better get very tough very fast. He decides he wants to be called "Kimo" - the name of Tully's boy. He smiles more, spends more time with his friends, and slowly becomes a kid. I'm not sure he ever had time before to just play. He begins to cheer up, laughs occasionally, and dwells more on the future than the past. I am beginning to think he just might make it in this country.

I buy him a bicycle. This one is a ten-speed and much faster than the models in Vietnam. He loves to go as fast as possible but control is not his strong point. I witness some truly spectacular crashes as he hits the curb and flies yards through the air. He becomes a constant patchwork of pink Band-Aids and dark skin. Now that he is thirteen he eats like a horse and begins to fill out.

One afternoon I watch him through the window. He walks over to a large open field across from the apartment. Suddenly he kicks off his sandals and begins to run. He runs through the grass and warm Arkansas air with arms up like airplane wings. He runs in huge circles, on and on. Finally he gives a summersault and flops into the grass on his back. He lies there, looking at the sky and toying with a blade of grass. It is the first time I've seen him act like a kid. In Vietnam, poverty, a large family and culture kept him working to help his family. I doubt that he had free time to lay in the grass and think. That is the moment I decide that I am content to have him with me. Youth and resiliency go hand in hand and seem to be working on him.

He and I go from a point of liking each other to a certain degree of affection. It is not a deep affection but comfortable for us both. We enjoy each other's company. He brings his buddies to the apartment to have me translate the really thorny issues in a 13 year old's life. He begins to describe me to his friends as his *"Fadder."* I like having a kid around, watching him learn and develop a new personality. I like this situation and am glad I allowed it to happen.

I take him to an Indian cultural center in Oklahoma. As our small group of tourists walk around the area with the Indian guide I softly translate the guide's explanation. The guide turns to me and asks, *"What tribe is he from?"* Kimo finds this greatly amusing. He buys a Indian headband and wears it constantly. His taste in clothes never changes. He still picks out the worst combination of colors and patterns imaginable. He asks me if the reason that people stare at him is because he is from Asia. The explanation that perhaps his green striped shirt and red plaid pants are sucking the eyes out of their heads strikes him as silly. He thinks he looks great.

In August the school year begins. We go to the local school to enroll him. The school has no other refugees at this point and no non-English speaking students. They see him as a challenge and do everything possible to help him. They place him in the seventh grade. Not surprisingly, he is a terrible student but very popular with the other kids and the teachers. He is thrilled to be liked by all these American kids. In Vietnam he was in a small minority and mostly ignored by the Vietnamese students in his school and neighborhood. He turns from a quiet, somewhat dour boy into a generally happy, smiling, often impish young man. Life is good, perhaps for the first time. He is growing like a weed and is now almost as tall as I am. Like most Cambodians, he is not the typical thin Asian and is quite sturdy. Vitamins, an American diet, sunshine, and exercise make him the picture of health.

Kimo appears to be coping with all this change and shows signs of adapting well. I think that he will be able to succeed, become self-supporting and integrate into America. He rarely mentions

Tully now and never speaks of Vietnam or his family. He becomes more of a little brother than a son. I like it. He revels in the fact that most American kids don't care if he is from Cambodia or the moon.

In September I take him to the dentist for a checkup. I doubt that he has ever seen a dentist before. His teeth are fine but need cleaning. I sit in the waiting room reading a magazine. Soon the dentist comes out with a worried look.

"Mr. Kassebaum, his gums are bleeding and I can't get it to stop."

"Don't gums usually bleed when you clean teeth?"

"Yes – but this isn't normal. I think you should take him the hospital. He has something wrong that should be seen by a doctor."

This doesn't worry me much. He is a strong kid, so far never sick.

"I'll call the hospital and tell them you are coming," says the dentist.

Kimo comes out of the treatment room. He looks fine.

"How do you feel?"

"Fine. But I'm swallowing blood."

"The dentist says we should stop at the hospital and have a doctor look at your mouth."

"Why?" He looks a little irritated. He has other plans for the afternoon.

"I don't think it will take more than a few minutes. The doctor will make the bleeding stop."

We leave the dentist and drive over to the hospital. Kimo keeps saying he is fine. We arrive at the Emergency Room where a young doctor is waiting for us. The dentist has, indeed, called ahead. He asks Kimo to sit on the examining table while he inspects his mouth. Kimo clearly thinks this whole trip is a waste of time. He draws some blood and asks him to pee in a cup. This request amuses and mystifies Kimo. We are asked to wait a few minutes while they run some tests on the specimens. We sit in the small waiting room.

A few minutes later the doctor is back. He comes right to the point.

"He has almost no white blood cells — 1% of normal. I don't know why just now but he's wide open to any infection. He should be admitted to the hospital right now."

"But he hasn't been the least bit sick!"

"If he leaves here now he is going to be very sick very quickly.

He will catch anything he comes into contact with."

I am not sure how to handle this. In Vietnam a hospital is considered to be a place to go to die – not to get well. I explain to Kimo that he needs to stay there for a night while they try to find out what is wrong with him. This upsets him greatly and he protests again that nothing is wrong with him.

"I hope nothing is wrong. But we need to be sure."

A nurse comes and escorts us up to the fourth floor. They have a sealed room with air locks and filters to reduce the chance of contact with stray germs. Fortunately it doesn't look too imposing or different. The nurse asks him to change into the typical backless hospital clothes. Kimo doesn't like this at all. The nurse suggests that I bring him his pajamas from home. I explain my short departure to him and leave.

When I return a few minutes later, Kimo has a ring of nurses around his bed and is clearly enjoying all the attention. He steps into the bathroom adjoining the room, puts on the bottoms of his pajamas as he does at home, and returns to hop up onto the bed. I show him the TV controls and other equipment, such as the call button for the nurses. He is worried and decides to bury his nose in the TV, rather than talk about this. When he falls asleep, I go back to the apartment.

The next morning I return to the hospital to find the doctors preparing Kimo for a bone marrow sample. He and the staff are unable to communicate. I ask the doctors to please not run tests like this before I can explain things to Kimo. This test requires pushing a needle into his hipbone and removing a small amount of marrow. It is short but painful. Kimo lies on his side, staring at the wall, and shows little emotion. Sometimes he can be VERY Asian.

An hour later, the doctor comes to visit. His news is grim. Kimo has aplastic anemia. For some unknown reason, Kimo's bone marrow no longer produces white blood cells to combat infection. He is vulnerable to any disease, no matter how minor. Without these defenses, he will succumb to any infection he develops. The only treatment in 1975 is highly experimental. The doctor asks if he and I had been exposed to Agent Orange.[3] Bone marrow transplants are being tested but the technology to match donors does not yet exist. The only possible donors are his closest relatives. The doctors have already contacted the International Red Cross to see if they could locate Kimo's family in Vietnam. The Vietnamese Government never responded. In the interim, there is little choice but for Kimo to become another "boy in the bubble."

By the third day, Kimo pleads to go home. He does not feel sick,

---

3

     Agent Orange was a chemical used to destroy the foliage that the Viet Cong often hid under. In my province of An Xuyen, wide strips were sprayed on the theory that the enemy could be seen moving from strip to strip. We all were exposed.

is frightened, and misses his friends. His friends are wonderful. He has a steady stream of 13 and 14 year olds that came to the hospital, go through the elaborate disinfecting procedures and spend time with him.

I ask the doctors if he could leave the hospital for a day.

"Look, Mr. Kassebaum, that is only in the movies. Kimo is vulnerable to anything and it would be like you or I drinking and swimming in polluted water."

By the fifth day, doctors say that Kimo's chances for survival are practically nonexistent. He looks perfectly normal and complains that he does not feel sick. Under these circumstances, the doctors fill him with every antibiotic they have and let him go home for one day. Kimo knows it is only for a day but is overjoyed. We go back to the apartment. My mother, always there for a crisis, has come to stay with us both. She stays with him while I go to buy groceries. Kimo has a steady stream of kids visiting and is very happy.

When I return, my mother is looking sad and the place is very quiet. After Kimo's friends left, he sat next to my mother and began to cry.

"Doctor say I die."

Obviously, one of the doctors discussed his case in front of him, not realizing that he could understand some English. I go to his room and find him sitting with a bad nosebleed. I was warned about this and so, after only a few hours at home, we head back to the hospital. Kimo is resigned to it and seems to know that this is his last trip.

He pauses for a moment in the parking lot to look around, sighed deeply and climbs into the car. We don't speak on the trip. At the hospital, he changes back into the hospital clothes, climbs up on his bed, and says little.

Blood transfusions begin and, over the next two days, over 40 pints of blood pass into his arm and almost directly back out from the nosebleed. Nonetheless, he still feels fine. He knows he is dying and his will to resist is ebbing. He stares out the window often as if he could see his familiar world of Vietnam, family, and other Cambodian boys. Instead he sees the first snow of the year - the first he has ever seen. He has been looking forward to seeing and touching it for the first time.

I spend the next five days with him at the hospital, only leaving to sleep. Tom O'Dell covers at the office. Kimo doesn't feel bad, except for the needle in his arm connected to the blood transfusions. He receives a steady flow. Where it all goes is a mystery to me. He puts on a good front, smiling and having good conversations with his frequent teenage visitors. After the fifth day with no change in his condition, I go back to the camp to catch up. My mother stays with him.

Around noon, my mother calls. *"You better come,"* is all she says. The hospital is only a few minutes away. When I enter the room, nurses and doctors surround Kimo. He is not conscious. My mother tells me that he was watching TV when he turned and said, *"I have headache."* He leaned back and my mother called the nurse.

I can only watch. The doctor, a young man about my age, calls me out into the hall.

"He has had a massive brain hemorrhage. All his responses are gone." We sit down and discuss what can be done. The doctor is as gentle as he can be but tells me the truth. *"The damage is done and is not reversible. His heart beats and he breathes but he will never regain consciousness. We can keep him alive for awhile but he will never know the difference. Or we can let nature take its course and see that he is comfortable. It's your decision."*

Strangely, the decision is not difficult. I am surprised to hear this in a Catholic hospital. I'm not sure I even have the right to make this decision. But if I don't make it, perhaps nobody will.

"Let him go, then."

I go back and look at him. He is a good-looking thirteen-year-old who looks strong and fit. He lies quietly looking as if he is sleeping. The doctor returns and suggests that I sit outside. My mother is a stronger person than I am. She stays with him.

After an hour, I begin to hear Kimo cough. The doctor comes out and assures me that it is only reflex and not an indication that he is conscious or aware.

"His lungs are filling with fluids. He isn't aware of it or in pain." The coughing continues for a time. I don't know how long. Each time I hear it, it is worse. Finally, it stops. The doctor comes out and lays his hand on my arm.

"I'm sorry," is all that he says.

Kimo is dead.

An American Buddhist monk holds his funeral service at Fort Chaffee. He is cremated, as are most Buddhists. Someday his ashes will go home, hopefully to his family. (Twenty-five years later I scatter some of his ashes in the Pacific Ocean, some on the mountain near the house and some over the graves of my parents. Finding his family has been impossible.)

Bung came thousands of miles, leaving his mother, father, brothers and sisters. At the time he jumped on the boat, I don't think he realized how final his actions would be. It was a childish thing to do, with no real thought about the consequences, but he was, after all, a child. The realization that he could not go home and that Tully would not take him had been difficult. He had not left Vietnam to live with me. We were thrown together by circumstances and we made the best of it. I was not his father and he was not my son. His real family had been large and poor. He didn't get much from them.

Kimo wouldn't know the impact that his short life would have on others. Because of him, other boys would have the course of their lives greatly altered. Certainly my life changed dramatically. He would have been proud of this.

Perhaps he does know.

I like to think so.

My work had to go on. The goal was to have all 50,000 sponsored and out of the camp by then end of the year – 1975. By December the camp was down to a small number of problem cases. Single young men, mostly ex-soldiers with no job skills, were difficult to place. The last person out was a former Saigon journalist who decided that the Untied States was responsible for his situation. He announced that he would stay in the camp and be supported by the government for the rest of his life. On December 31 the M.P.s handcuffed him, drove him to the bus station in Little Rock, gave him a ticket to Chicago along with directions to his sponsor, and then left him. Fort Chaffee was put back into mothballs.

In the final weeks of the camp, A.I.D. decided that they no longer needed the CORDS people who had no skills in regular work performed by their agency. There were eleven A.I.D./CORDS people at Chaffee and A.I.D. fired nine of them by terminating their contracts. I remained because I had been reclassified by Hank Cushing some years earlier into a standard A.I.D. job classification. At the time it meant nothing to me since I did not even understand the distinction and obviously did not do that type work. Fortunately, Hank Cushing did. It saved my career.

In January 1976 I reported to the Foreign Service Institute to study Spanish before my posting to Colombia. I was only there for two weeks when a cable from the Mission in Colombia asked that I come immediately. I thought it was really nice to go from unwanted to desperately needed in one month. Little did I know.

Colombia

I arrived in Bogota as a very young senior officer still reeling from Kimo's death. After almost 7 years in the Foreign Service I had not worked a single day for A.I.D.. The Mission had about 30 Americans in it, all 10 to 20 years older than I. I was Deputy (Thank God!) Director of the Program Office, the office that supervises and approves all activities in the Mission. In 48 hours I knew two things for a fact: 1.) I didn't have a clue what I was doing and 2) with the exception of my boss and the Deputy Mission Director, the entire Mission hated my guts! When introduced for the first time to the Controller, Jerry Martin, he told me *"I have no use for any of you who were in Viet-Nam and you all should be fired!"* And he was the friendly one.

The Director of the Program Office was George McClosky. George was a good man and understood my problems. He intended to teach and turn me into a Program Officer during my two year tour. Without George I probably would have either resigned or been fired. Phil Schwab was the Deputy Mission Director who, in fact, ran the Mission. He too was a kind and sympathetic friend. Phil had his own cross to bear. The Mission Director was a political appointee named James Magellas. Appointed by Vice-President Hubert Humphrey, Magellas had no talent, interest, or experience in A.I.D. He liked to make speeches and often made promises that were impossible or illegal to implement. Poor Phil Schwab had to follow him and clean up the mess.

Magellas was the one who insisted that I arrived immediately. This had nothing to do with work. Mission Directors' salaries are increased in larger Missions. Magellas would have his salary cut if I did not show up to keep the number up. Two months after I arrived, A.I.D. decided to close down the Colombia Mission. With no new programs planned it gave George and I a lot of teaching time. (George had five children, each with a genetic disorder causing them to be deaf by their teenage years. George died a few years after I left Colombia, leaving three kids still at home.)

The Mission had projects in health but the largest programs by far were anti-narcotic efforts to stem the flow of cocaine to the United States. The health projects were visible – the narcotics projects were not.

Dr. Tom Hyslop, a contractor, managed the population control project. A.I.D. recognized that overpopulation was a serious problem in most developing countries. Until the religious rightwingers in the U.S. became involved, A.I.D. had programs around the world to supply condoms and birth control devices to the poor. In Colombia even some Catholic priests supported the effort. One priest working in the slums of Bogota included in every sermon this message; *'Just because you have all the children that you can afford and care for is no reason for you to go to the clinic down on the corner where they will show you how to prevent more children that you cannot afford or care for. Especially do not go between the hours of 9 and 5 when they are open!"*

I didn't have a great deal of work in the population project beyond managing the funds for it.

The anti-narcotics projects were mostly clandestine. The U.S. Army, through SOUTHCOM in Panama, had Special Forces troops operating with the Colombian Army. Unknown to the Colombians they also sometimes operated without the knowledge of the Colombians. Officially all US troops in the country were attached to Colombian military units and they had no headquarters or other offices. A.I.D. funneled money to the Summer Institute for Linguistics, an organization founded to translate the Bible into indigenous languages. Publicly they sent missionaries into the jungle to live with Indian tribes, learn their language and write the Bible for them. Perhaps somebody actually did this but I never saw any results.

The Summer Institute for Linguistics/Colombia was a front and received millions of dollars from the CIA, funneled through A.I.D. The Summer Institute for Linguistics armed and trained the indigenous groups into guerilla fighters to combat the narco-trafficers that encroached into their lands. These Indian groups also resisted the Columbian government's efforts to take their lands. The Summer Institute for Linguistics operated so far from civilization that the Colombian government had little idea what they were doing. Neither did we.

I signed off on millions of dollars for the Summer Institute for Linguistics. Beyond that I wanted nothing to do with the mostly useless and ineffective program. The problem of narcotics 30 years later is no less than in 1976. Based on information that the Summer Institute decided to pass on to me, and I then passed on to SOUTHCOM, the US Special Forces would occasionally operate deep in the jungle without the knowledge of the Colombians.

One area of Colombia that was so remote and primitive that the Colombian government rarely even attempted to govern was the province of Choco. Choco lies on the border with Panama and had no roads, industry, commercial agriculture or public services. The area is so swampy that even the narcotics growers had no interest. A.I.D. had invested in small projects over the years but had never visited any of them to see if the money was properly spent. I decided to go see them. I spent a week traveling by boat to villages that looked as if they were in Africa. The people were black — the descendants of escaped slaves back in the 16th and 17th centuries. They hid in Choco and recreated their homes in Africa. It was a fascinating trip.

With the A.I.D. Mission closing down, no new projects to design and an ever decreasing workload as old projects ended, I had a lot of free time. Between the narcotics problems and the various anti-government revolutionary movements much of the country was unsafe. Once I felt that I had learned as much as possible about A.I.D. I asked for an early transfer. The Mission Director, still fearing a cut in salary, refused to forward it. In some respects, Colombia was a nice long vacation.

One important thing did happen while I was working in Colombia. The Foreign Service had for many years kept some people untenured for decades. After the collapse of Viet-Nam they quite legally fired dozens of people who had worked for as long as 19 years without tenure. They usually received no benefits or pension. Congress addressed this with a new law giving the Foreign Service five years to either tenure or separate new employees. With more than five years of service I was automatically tenured and now had some job security.

There was not one other person in the Embassy in Colombia that had served in Vietnam. I had no desire to talk about it but there is a peculiar effect that surfaces after years in a war zone. I *missed* the war, it was my worst of times, my best of times, in some ways the time of my life. Hunkered down in a bunker or laying on the side of a mud fort while bullets flew every direction, I had never felt more alive. I had to do something.

With little else to do, I continue to tour the country to inspect A.I.D. projects. The rest of the A.I.D. staff has little interest in this and it gives me a great way to really see the country – at least the safe parts.

It took a couple of months for my car to arrive in the port of Barranquilla. Usually one of the chauffeurs would be sent to the port to pick it up. I decided to go with the driver. Roads in Colombia are often poorly marked so that it was probably not a good idea for me to go alone. To make the trip more productive, I compiled a list of A.I.D. projects along the route to inspect on the trip back to Bogota. One project was in Ibague.

Ibague is a medium-sized town on the high side of the Andes Mountains. It is more modern than most Colombian towns of its size. It is warm in the days and cool at night. Snow usually covers the nearby peaks.

I have breakfast in the morning and meet Alphonso, the driver, in front of the hotel. We find the car and start for the morning's work. Usually I drive but today Alphonso knows where we are going. I read the file on the school we are to visit. Albergue Infantil Alphonso Lopez is not actually a school. It is an orphanage operated by the local Lions Club. It takes only boys between the ages of 6 and 14 and receives food from A.I.D. to help feed its residents.

As we pull onto the grounds, I see the main building at the top of a small hill. It is concrete with metal windows. The metal window frames are a bit rusty and the concrete of the building is flaking a bit but by local standards it is not a bad looking place, although rather small for 125 kids to live in.

We pull in and park. The entrance is on the backside of the building. As I walk around to the office, I can see a large concrete pad. The side of the building is decorated with a large mural of child-like painting of local scenes. From here I can see that the school is actually almost a square composed of several identical concrete buildings. Between the buildings is a garden with many large plants. About 20 boys rapidly collect around us. They are raucous and full of energy but mostly just curious. Obviously they don't see many visitors.

In the office, the woman who is director of the orphanage is surprised by the visit but not displeased. She shows me the storage area for the A.I.D. food, the kitchen where it is prepared and gives me a short tour of the school. The place is clean and well maintained but the wear and tear of many active boys is evident.

After the tour, the Director asks me to her quarters for a cold drink. While we talk, boys hang through the open windows and peer through the door.

"I noticed as we walked around that there are very few adults here. How many people work here?" I asked.

"Most of the time I am here and a few others may show up." She explains that many of the boys here are not orphans. They attend the 'school' and are fed by the kitchen. Their mothers rotate the work to cook the food and look after the boys during

the day in return for the education and food their sons receive. About half of the 125 boys leave in the evening.

"How many boys were adopted here in the last year?" I ask.

The Director gives a short laugh. *"None! I've been working here for 14 years and seen one boy adopted. He went to Switzerland."*

I was still recovering from Kimo's death and had given some thought to just how much I had enjoyed the experience with him. As we talked I told the Director that I was considering the adoption of a boy. This came out of the blue and even surprised me! She knew an opportunity when she saw it.

"I'll line up the boys you can adopt. You need to know which ones are day students and which ones are adoptable. I'll show you the ones you can choose from."

I'm horrified. The idea of lining up the orphans and walking down the line, like a general reviewing the troops, is too much. Perhaps she thinks I will pick out a few for interviews and the final cut. With explanations that I've not really made up my mind yet, I exit flustered but as gracefully as I can.

Back in Bogota, Theresa Bocanegra, the local A.I.D. lawyer, becomes a daily visitor to my office. I made the mistake of mentioning that I had considered adoption and asking her about the Colombian adoption laws. I may not have made up my mind but she has made up hers. While I have not committed to adopting any child, she suggests I adopt two!

After a great deal of thought, I decide that I'm going to at least explore the possibilities. And Theresa is right – two should be easier than one. I still have a job and will need to be absent at times. Two boys will better entertain themselves than one. I tell Theresa about my visit to Ibague. To my surprise, she not only knows all the players in the Ibague Bienestar Familiar (Department of Welfare), she also knows the Director that I met. Theresa is ready to go. I am less willing to begin anything until I know that I can carry the entire process to its conclusion.

I meet with the Immigration Officer at the Embassy. He explains that my copy of the Virginia code is useful, but that he needs a letter from the Virginia authorities to approve any adoption. Once again, I think this is the end of this road.

I write to Richmond and receive a letter stating that they will not approve an adoption by a single man. I call them – not easy in those days. We have an unpleasant and formal conversation. I rewrite my letter to them asking them to state which provisions of the Virginia code prohibit me from adopting.

No answer.

I follow this with another letter demanding an answer to the last. Finally I receive a cold, somewhat nasty response consisting of two pages explaining that the "policy" of the

Virginia Department of Social Welfare is to not approve adoptions by single people. The final line, however, admits that there is no legal prohibition preventing me from qualifying as an adopter as long as I adopt male children. Petulantly, they state that they "cannot prevent an adoption taking place overseas." Our I.N.S. man is satisfied with this.

The adoption business in Colombia is corrupt and squeezes every cent out of prospective foreign adoptions. Under Colombian law, every orphan in the country under the age of 12 months technically belongs to the Bogota capitol district, regardless of the child's location. The President's sister operated that system. I am not interested in infants.

With Theresa pushing me, I decide to try the orphanage in Ibague a second time – but on my terms this time. Theresa calls the Director and explains that I would like to come back a second time to look at children but *"please, don't let the children know why he is there."* The Director agrees.

In March, 1976, Theresa and I arrange to return to Ibague and the orphanage. I've told the Director of the orphanage that I would like to see boys between the ages of 6 and 8. Younger isn't a problem – the orphanage doesn't have boys below age six. Older seems risky to me — too much personality already formed. Theresa is really into this business now. I am frankly very nervous about this trip. For me, this is the final point of backing out. One nod of the head on this trip and I'm down a path of no return. I have decided that, if I start this process, then, by God, I'll finish it. No way can I do to any child what I saw Tully do to Kimo.

Theresa and I arrive and are escorted into some sort of clinic room by the Director. About 30 boys enter the room and line up in rows on the far side of the room. They all look to be at least ten years old. The other boys are again hanging through the windows. Theresa tells me that the boys have been told I'm some sort of government inspector. Yeah, right. A government inspector that doesn't speak very good Spanish.

Having arranged this, I now have absolutely no idea what to do. They all look like, well, boys. The members of the group are tall, short, black, white and every other color. Theresa and the Director are whispering.

Theresa says, *"That one in the back on the left is a nice boy."* (How she knows this is a mystery.)

"How old is he?"

"We don't know," responds the Director.

I still don't know what to do and am beginning to wish I hadn't started this. The Director notices that I have a camera. She asks me if I will take photos of some of the boys.

"They need ID cards and must have photos. We don't have money for this. Could you?"

The perfect escape. I head (flee?) out the door to buy black and white film down the street. Theresa follows. While we are doing this, Theresa has a non-stop line about choosing two of the boys. I don't really listen – I've screwed myself by insisting that the boys do not know why I am there. Now I don't have any way to make a judgment.

I buy the film and, with a feeling of dread, return to the orphanage with Theresa. The Director has selected about ten boys for photos. I pick a white wall outside to shoot against.

The Director shoos away the other boys. One by one, I place the chosen boys against the wall and take a close-up photo. One of the boys is the one Theresa had pointed at in the Clinic. (Those pictures are now prized possessions although Allan and James hate them.)

On the drive back Theresa talks incessantly about all of this but

I'm not listening. I leave Theresa at her home and go back to my house.

At this point, I'm 49% ready to forget the whole thing. I have no idea how to select the "right" boys. Maybe I'm not up to making a decision this important. I should not have worried; as it turned out, I really had no say in the decision of whom I selected.

The next night my phone rings. It is the Director. My Spanish, after 4 months of private lessons in spare time, is just barely adequate.

"Senor, what did you think?"

"I know these kids need homes but they all look much older than 8. I don't know."

"OK. I'll find the right age for you." Click.

The next night: *"Senor, how about 13 and 11 years old?"*

"No. Too old."

The next night: *"12 and 10?"*

"Too old."

And yet the next night: *"11 and 9?"*

"Still too old! No."

And another night: *"How about 10 and 8?"*

"OK – OK! I'll look."

The next weekend, I return to Ibague – this time without Theresa. Again I've asked the Director to not tell the boys why I am there. It just doesn't seem right to tell them they are being inspected for adoption. Not when it might not work out.

The two boys are playing in the courtyard and are unaware of me as I look out a window nearby. All the boys saw my car arrive but lost interest when I disappeared into the Director's quarters. This time she shut the door and windows. I ask the Director, *"What are their names?"*

"The taller one is Alirio. The other is Jaime." Alirio is the one pointed out to me in the clinic. I remember his face from the photos I took.

"I thought you didn't know his age."

"Well, I didn't at the time but I looked it up in the records. He's ten and the other one is eight."

Even allowing for malnutrition, these boys looked big for their ages. *"Are you sure?"*

"Oh, yes. It's in the records."

We step outside. Boys congregate instantly. To my surprise,

the Director shoos them and they move away and lose interest. One thing was clear – the Director has decided that these are the boys I should take.

"Why do you think these are the boys I should adopt?" This is blunt but I want to know. She thinks about it for a minute. She waves at a nearby boy to come over.

She asks the boy, *"Do you have a brother here?"*

"Si, Senora."

"Who is your brother?"

"I forget," he says. She waves him away.

"See," she says. *"Of all these boys, Alirio and Jaime are among the few that stick together. Any boy who picks on one has a fight with both. I admire them because they always take care of each other."* She pauses. *"These are the boys you want."*

I'm often uncomfortable with the Director. At times I feel as if I'm in a pet store. She talks about the children with them standing right in front of her. It embarrasses me. What do you say to a 10 or 12 year that old you are considering? *"How would you like to be my kid?"* These kids cling to any adult – me, Theresa, the Director. They are malnourished and thin, starved for affection as well as decent food.

Deep breath. *"Ok, I'll do it."*

She broke into a wide grin. *"You can take them back to Bogota right now."*

"What?"

"You can take them with you now."

Whoa, Nellie! Things are going waaaay too fast.

"I can't do that. I don't have any assurance that this is going to work. I have to have some form of legal custody. I can't take these boys now and then bring them back if some paperwork doesn't work out. No, not now. And please – don't tell them anything until I know for sure."

I call Theresa at her home. She indeed knows everything, including my concerns. She assures me that she will take care of all the paperwork – and quickly. In a few days everything is arranged.

Beryl is a friend who speaks excellent Spanish and has accompanied me. As I pull onto the orphanage grounds and slowly climb the small hill, I decide that I'm way past the time to worry about this decision. As usual, all the boys flood out of the buildings to see what is happening.

By the time I park, the Director is standing by the building with Alirio and Jaime beside her. They are wearing clean but old T-shirts, pants and shoes. The other boys are running around noisily. We get out of the car.

"They are ready, senor." Both boys are smiling but I can't really detect their emotions about all this. The Director and I have a short conversation. She knows that it is a long drive back to Bogota and understands when I tell her that I think it is best if we leave quickly.

I open the car door and the two boys climb into the back seat. It is a well-stuffed Pinto. The boys have no good-byes for anybody and seem excited about leaving. I do not notice that they have brought nothing with them. So far, the two boys have said nothing. As we approach the gate, Alirio leans forward between the seats and asks Beryl, *"What do we call him?"* as he points at me.

I never thought about this. What <u>are</u> they going to call me?

Beryl laughs and says, *"Why don't you call him Papa. That's what he is going to be."*

"So when did you know I was coming to get you?" I ask.

"About an hour ago," replies Alirio.

"What did the Director tell you?"

"That a gringo was coming to adopt us."

"And what did you think?"

"That's good," he replies somewhat neutrally.

I take this short response to mean that he is reserving his opinion for awhile – a natural reaction.

When I ask Jaime a few questions, each time he turns and looks at Alirio – who answers for him. Clearly Jaime has more fears and worries about this than Alirio.

In Bogota, I drop Beryl off at her house and we head home. The boys are quiet – and tired. At the house they meet the maid, who disappears into her quarters. She left something on the table for us to eat.

I finally notice that they have brought nothing with them. *"Do you have any other clothes?"* I ask.

"No, Papa," Alirio answers, *"The Director said we would have plenty of clothes here and they need clothes for the boys at the orphanage."* At least the "Papa" thing went well.

The next morning we are off to the doctor. Dr. Castro received his medical degree in Kentucky and had practiced there for years. When the Colombian government set up a program to encourage Colombian doctors to come home, he returned. He was good doctor and would also understand all of us. I needed complete physicals for the boys for several reasons. First to see what their health problems were and, second, to make sure that my health insurance company could not claim "pre-existing conditions" and refuse to pay any future claims.

The doctor examines Allan first. Allan and I have agreed that this will be his new name.

"His age?"

"I don't know. I thought you might be able to tell me." The doctor knew the situation when I made the appointment.

He gives Allan a good examination, draws some blood, and asks him to pee in a bottle.

"I guess he is at least 12 years old. He's in pretty good shape – just underweight."

So much for "ten years old." And James wasn't his twin.

He moves on to James. (His agreed-upon new name.) He guesses that James is about 10 years old. The exam goes well until the time to draw a blood sample. James shuts his eyes, grimaces, but holds still while the needle goes into his arm. The doctor withdraws blood slowly so that it will not be more painful than necessary. Finally, James opens his eyes and looks at his arm. Seeing the needle and the blood, his eyes flutter briefly and then he slides slowly to the floor. I might have been more upset if Dr. Castro did not find this so amusing. Holding the needle, the doctor went right down to floor with James and finishes the job.

We lay James on the examining table and he revives. He is all right, just frightened. According to the doctor, James is very underweight. He weighs 44 pounds – 75 is about normal. The doctor's prescription for both is simple – feed them.

We return to the doctor a few days later for the test results. Dr. Castro explains that the tests are all negative for Allan. He is underweight and has a weak knee but he has no real problems. He does need a dentist badly and to have one leg in a cast for a few weeks. Then he hands me a two page single-spaced list of Latin words with James' name at the top.

"This is the list of internal parasites found in James. Even here in Colombia, I've never seen some of these before. It certainly explains why he is so thin. He's feeding quite a population there."

"Good God, what do we do?"

"Relax. Nothing there is dangerous or incurable. It just will take some time."

For the next six weeks, they take daily doses of various things to clear out the parasites. It does wonders for them both. They rapidly lose the skinny look, pack on some weight, and soon look like normal kids their ages.

When we go to the dentist, we all get a surprise. The dentist had a Ph.D. from New York University in Anthropology. He quickly discovered that there was little possibility in making a living in this field and switched to dentistry. In his spare time he identified the origins of Colombian Indian mummies, usually from teeth. There are thousands of mummies in the high, dry and cold Andes Mountains.

He turns to me and says in English, *"You're not their father."*

Brilliant — two Colombian boys and an obviously American. I explain the situation. He proceeds. *"This boy is a Pijao Indian."* He goes to his office and returns with some 8 x 10 rather disgusting photos of mummies. He points out tooth characteristics that I can't see but are clear to him.

After this long English conversation Allan asks what we are talking about. The dentist switches to Spanish and says, *"You are a Pijao Indian."*

"No, I am not!!"

"Yes, you are."

"No, I'm not."

"I'll tell you where you were born," says the dentist. *"Near the town of Ibague."*

"My father told you that."

Now it is my turn — *"No, I didn't."*

Allan and James are not happy. In Colombia, the Indians are the bottom of the social system.

Theresa Bocanegra spends many hours on the adoption. She refuses to consider any pay for her services. The people at the Bienestar Familiar in Ibague do all the papers and arrange for the courts. At that time the average cost for an adoption by a foreigner is around $5,000. They are aware of these prices but also refuse any offer of compensation. Allan and James are probably not aware that many people, some quite poor, work on their behalf for free. In spite of all these good intentions, however, I am worried. Allan and James have been with me for two months and nothing is official. We are becoming a family now and I could not bear to see a failure of the adoption process now.

Our life in Bogota settles into a routine. The boys go to the third grade in Collegio Rochester, a private English language school. I go to work and return as early as possible. We have a nice house in a good neighborhood. There are few Americans in the area but the boys' friends are mostly Colombians. They don't learn much English, or as Allan tells me, *"Why should I learn this strange language? You are the only person in the neighborhood that speaks it."* My attempts to convince them that few people will speak Spanish in the United States doesn't impress them.

The U.S. government closes the foreign aid operation in

Colombia about 18 months after my arrival. Colombia has reached a standard and no longer qualifies as an underdeveloped country. This was obviously a decision made by somebody who never left the center of Bogota. I take Allan and James to as many places as possible during this time. It is unlikely that they will ever return to their birthplace. With the exceptions of the Native Americans in the United States, we Americans are all the descendants of other places and cultures. The boys have real roots of thousands of years in Colombia. Kicking and usually protesting, I drag the boys from one Pijao cultural site to another. Allan and James are a tiny remnant of an entire race whose culture was destroyed by the Spanish in their greed for the gold the Pijaos crafted into wonderful art. Their culture was destroyed three hundred years ago. In another hundred years, there will be no pure Pijaos left. They will have vanished from the face of the earth.

When my two year tour was finished in January 1979 the three of us packed up and went to Washington. The expensive and clandestine war against the drug lords had little impact. There was far too little money to have much impact in other programs. I was not sorry to go.

D.C.

In 1979 A.I.D. was still a large agency with about 10,000 people. It had entire office buildings in DC, Virginia and Maryland. About 80% of the employees in the US were civil servants who occupied and jealously guarded their positions. Foreign Service Officers were seen – rightly – as temporary desk holders waiting for their next overseas assignment. The level of bureaucracy was difficult to understand, especially for somebody like me that had operated independently for years. I once wrote a telegram of no particular importance and it required 35 clearances! When it finally came back with all the approvals I threw it into the trash. So much time had been consumed that it no longer was needed.

At home Allan and James were struggling in school. James was in the 4th grade barely able to understand the English. He had a good and sympathetic teacher who took the time to help him and he gradually improved. He was fortunate that he had the same teacher all day.

Allan was placed in the 7th grade in a special class for non-English speakers – with 28 Vietnamese! After a few hours he was bussed to Chantilly High School and placed in regular classes. He had a different teacher for each class. He complained that the special class spoke Vietnamese most of the time and that his other teachers simply did not have the time to give him any extra help. The school system was failing to help him.

In October, Hank Cushing called me and asked if I would switch to the State Department and the Boat People Refugee program. It seems that the State Department had released its entire Vietnamese language qualified people after the war ended. Now they needed Vietnamese-speaking Consular Officers to process the boat people and to collect intelligence from them. I knew that the American Schools overseas were far better than the Fairfax system and would give Allan and James the attention they needed and, well, I was bored out of my mind in DC. I jumped at the chance.

Hank's first offer would have been a dream a few years earlier. He offered to send me to Malaysia because I spoke both Vietnamese and Malay. The job meant that Allan and James would live in Kuala Lumpur and I would spend *"28 days a month on the beaches and in the camps – and getting TDY money the whole time!"*

Hank thought it strange that I didn't find this offer appealing. I turned it down because I could not leave Allan and James to live with a housekeeper.

Hank's next offer was Singapore. *"You can live in Singapore. The camps are in Indonesia on nearby islands. There isn't any place to live near the camps so you would commute each day back to Singapore."* I accepted.

Singapore

I left Allan and James with my parents in Oklahoma. It would give them some time to visit and I would have a week or so to find a place to live and get them registered into the school.

Everything that could go wrong did.

As is the usual practice in all countries, the Singapore government's permission was needed for me to be posted there. They had no problem with my posting. However, they, and the Embassy, assumed that my status as 'single' meant that only one person would arrive. Today, of course, few people would make that assumption but in 1979 there were few single parents. Either they overlooked Allan and James or the Embassy forgot to tell them. Singapore had an agreement with the Soviet Union to allow both Embassies to have the same total number of people. Singapore was no fan of the Soviet Union but did have a considerable investment in businesses that overhauled the Russian fishing fleet. The Singapore government did not withdraw their approval for me but declined to issue visas for Allan and James. As one sympathetic Singapore Foreign Office official put it, *"With you we get two children, with the Russians we get two more spies."*

At first, the delays in visas for the two boys went unexplained or, more accurately, explained as just bureaucratic foot dragging. One week turned into two, then four, then six before I finally got a decent explanation. Meanwhile I had rented an apartment near the American School and proceeded as if the boys would be arriving soon.

I still had a job to do and each day I took a fast boat from the Singapore harbor to Tanjang Pinang, Indonesia. Tanjang Pinang was nothing more than a small fishing village. The office was a simple wooden shack in town with a desk and a telex machine. I heard consistent rumors from the people in town that the nearby refugee camp was a disaster – inadequate housing, sanitation, and food. My requests to visit the camp were turned down repeatedly by the Indonesian authorities on the basis that they had not completed an appropriate office for me to use.

I had received detailed instructions on the operation of the telex machine before my first visit to Indonesia. This large machine used spools of ribbon-like paper. You used the typewriter part of the thing to type out your message. The typewriter punched holes in the paper somewhat like Braille. To transmit the message you rewound the tape, inserted it into the side of this monstrous machine, and then dialed the receiving telex on the telephone. In those days of unreliable and very expensive international calls, the telex was designed to transmit the message very quickly at lower cost. My first report was quite lengthy. I dialed up the number given to me by the

Embassy in Jakarta. The telex shook and rattled as it ate up my tape. In a few moments I received an answer – *"Very interesting – but this is a bank in Luxembourg."*

After more than a month of stonewalling by the Indonesian authorities and a final explanation from the Singapore Foreign Office about visas for Allan and James, it was clear that this assignment would not work out. I called Washington to request either a transfer to another refugee post where the boys would be with me or a switch back to A.I.D. My first call got nowhere. Hank Cushing was on vacation and only he could make this decision. I waited a few more days until after Hank was supposed to be back at work and called again. Hank had extended his vacation for another three weeks. I asked for his home phone number. The oddly nervous response was *"We don't know where he is."* I called a few friends in Washington but they had no luck in locating him either. Meanwhile Allan and James' short visit with their grandparents was beginning to look like something much longer. They even began the school year at the local school. This simply would not do.

Hank and his wife of perhaps 25 years, Hazel, were in the process of divorcing with some acrimony. I liked them both. Finally I called Hazel and explained the situation and asked if she knew how to contact hank.

"Yes, I completely understand," she said. *"Here is a number where I am sure you can reach him."*

I called the number and Hank answered the phone. Before I could say much of anything he asked, *"How did you get this number?"* When I explained that I had tried his office, several mutual friends and then finally called his ex-wife, Hank went ballistic! We had a few minutes of shouting at each other with Hank telling me to never, ever talk with his ex-wife again and me telling him that he might pick my assignments but not my friends. (It turned out that the not-yet divorced Hank was living with his girlfriend and thought that absolutely nobody knew about it. Most of the people I had contacted did know but were afraid to say anything. Even his wife knew where he was!)

When calmness returned, Hank became his usual self. He understood the problem and offered me Hong Kong and Macau. I accepted. It took me a few days to arrange travel, cancel my apartment lease and depart.

Hong Kong and Macau

I arrived in Hong Kong and checked into a hotel and stopped by at the Consulate (As a British colony, we did not have a full embassy.). My first priority was to get Allan and James on a plane so that the three of us were back together. They arrived a few days later.

I enrolled them into the Hong Kong International School. This private school received a lot of money from the Consulate and had an agreement to take all American Consulate kids. At the same time, they had a policy to not accept any students, even in kindergarten, who were not fluent in English. The school was about 70% Chinese kids from very wealthy families that planned on their children going on to North American universities. The private British schools did not provide the proper entrance prerequisites.

Allan and James were the first American kids to come to the school that did not speak fluent English. James could cope with classes but Allan could not. The school decided to give him his own teacher with the single objective of teaching him English. Recognizing that this would probably be overwhelming, they also accepted another boy from the Malaysian Consulate who also needed to learn English. Allan's teacher was wonderful in spite of the comment, *"He will learn English in six months or drop dead in the process."* They placed him in grade 7. This angered Allan since Fairfax had promoted him to grade 8 in spite of learning practically nothing. Actually the number was irrelevant since he had few regular classes.

I think Allan now realized that he was more or less stuck with learning English. Even at home his brother would answer him in English, much to Allan's' disgust. Characteristically Allan then threw himself into the process with his usual determination and tenacity. Although he will never lose his strong accent (Sorry, son!) Allan today speaks better English than the majority of native-born Americans.

The Colony of Hong Kong was already crowded with some 5 million people when the outpouring of Vietnamese boat people

began. After 5 years of the People's Republic of Vietnam jailing those who tried to escape, they changed their policy (taking a lesson from fellow Communist Cuba) and decided to expel all those dissidents and trouble makers. This included the Chinese population that had not assimilated well.

As many as 30 overcrowded barely sea-worthy boats would arrive each day. Within a few months the population of refugees rose to over 100,000.

The British, hard-pressed to house the legitimate population, nonetheless did their best. They had refugees in warehouses, apartment buildings slated for demolition, airplane hangers and so on, scattered throughout the colony. The British were desperate for help to move them on to resettling countries. I worked with representatives from Canada, France, Germany, Spain, Japan, Greece, and even Brazil. As usual the United Nations High Commission for Refugees arrived, rented a large office, purchased some chauffeured cars, and did absolutely nothing productive.

I was soon joined by Anne Henshaw. A State Department lawyer, Anne did not speak Vietnamese but was fluent in martini. If she returned from lunch at all, she was generally drunk. More senior than I, she was the titular head of the office.

We recognized that I could not possible interview refugees in the numbers that we were willing to take. Anne could not interview any of them. Our budget, separate from the Consulate, to its displeasure, was generous. The Lutheran Church received a contract to conduct all the preliminary interviews, weed out the obviously unqualified, and collect much of the information I needed. These pre-interviews were conducted by a staff of around 100 Chinese North American college graduates. They were outstanding. This file in hand I could generally interview a family for a few minutes and make a decision.

In addition to moving as many qualified refugees to the US as possible, I had two other roles. First was to collect information about POWs (prisoners of war) and MIAs (missing in action and presumed, at that point, to be dead). The US was determined to bring home all of its war dead as was possible. Refugees quickly knew that, if they could provide accurate information about Americans in Vietnam, dead or alive, they would move to the head of the line. I was quickly flooded with information. Most of it was invented. I put out the word in the camps that accurate information moved the refugee and family to the head of the line and invented information to the back of the line. From that point I still received a lot of information that was false but recognized that the refugees really did usually believe their story. For example, one teenager told me he saw two Americans in Hanoi on the street waiting for a bus. Russians, but he didn't know the difference. This type of thing had no effect on their processing.

My other role was to collect intelligence on the internal affairs in Vietnam. It soon became obvious that the Communists were more interested in consolidating their power and reconstructing the economy of the country than in meddling in the neighboring country's affairs. I collected a lot of information of no importance and gave it little time.

At home the situation was becoming intolerable. We were living in a hotel, eating in restaurants, and the boys had no place to run. After 30 days my per diem was cut in half, after 30 more days, cut in half again. At this point I could no longer afford the bills in expensive Hong Kong. I had moved from a decent hotel to the cheapest safe place I could find. The Lok Wok Hotel was the setting for the movie, "The World of Suzy Wong." It had a nice staff but the place was so bad that we had to place newspapers on the floor so that the boys could stretch out and do their homework. The refugee program had lots of money for refugee operations but no money for our housing. With a separate budget from the Consulate, they had no money to provide us with a home. Even the boy's school tuition of US$30,000 was 'borrowed' from the Consulate. Washington continued to promise that housing money would be arriving 'soon.' When it did arrive it could not reimburse me for potentially thousands of dollars in personal debt for hotel bills. I rented a 'leave flat' for a few months but it still wasn't a home.

Reluctantly I went to see the Consul General, Tom Shoesmith. Shoesmith was sympathetic and grateful that I was adequately dealing with a situation that could have been a serious problem with the British. I had no choice but to tell him that I needed a stable and adequate place for my family or I needed to ask for a transfer. He also understood that Anne Henshaw would be unable to deal with anything.

He called in the Administrative Officer and asked if there were any empty Consular apartments. There were none.

"We have nothing?"

"Nothing."

With a bit of a grin, Shoesmith ordered the Admin. Officer, *"Give him the Charge d'affairs' old house."*

The Admin. Officer turned beet red but knew better than to argue. Washington had ordered the Consulate to move its entire staff into rented apartments. In crowded Hong Kong, most apartments are small and noisy. The Charge d'affair had already moved from his very large mansion on the peak and into a very large apartment near the Consulate.

The house was to be sold but the paperwork would probably take a year. Other than the Consul General's large and luxurious mansion on the peak, this house was the largest housing in the Consulate and one of the very few real houses in all of Hong Kong.

The boys and I moved. This house was enormous, with 20 foot ceilings, a dining room and table that could seat 30, 5 servant's apartments, a kitchen with two of every appliance, a huge living room, and, mysteriously, only two large bedrooms. The house also had what looked like a bell tower but actually contained a small room. James took the downstairs bedroom and Allan wanted the bell tower. I, of course, took the other downstairs bedroom.

I often entertained the refugee staff. All 100 could fit into this place. I was smart enough not to invite the other Consulate people.

I ask around through the Consulate grapevine for a housekeeper/cook. The first applicant is Joseph. He's about 40 years old, short, and wears thick glasses. His English is, well, strange.

"Where are you working now?" I ask.

"I a messenger."

"How long have you done this?"

"Three month."

"What did you do before that?"

"I at Chief of Surgery in hospital."

His experience as a cook? None. His experience as a housekeeper in a western house? None. Naturally I hire him. This is too interesting to pass up.

Hong Kong has peculiar laws. For Mainland Chinese who cross into Hong Kong illegally, and there are thousands, the border is not the real barrier. Gurka soldiers and the police heavily patrol the border. They capture the large majority of those attempting to enter the colony and return them directly to the Chinese authorities. Between the border and the actual colony lies the 99 square mile New Territories, an area leased to the British after the Boxer Rebellion. For those I.I.s (illegal immigrants who successfully cross the border, or arrive by sea), arrest in the New Territories still results in being returned to the Chinese authorities.

A few I.I.s make it through the New Territory to the colony proper. The colony consists of Hong Kong Island and a tiny portion of Kowloon on the mainland. Boundary Street is that official border. An I.I. who can penetrate this far into the colony can go to the nearest police station and receive papers to legalize his presence.

"Joseph" Mei Ling Tak actually had been the Chief of Surgery in a large hospital in Shanghai. In this capacity, he was invited to attend a conference of surgeons in Australia. The Chinese Government had approved the trip. Airline connections in Hong Kong required an overnight stay. Joseph got no further. He defected as soon as he exited the airport. (Australia has a strong 'no Asians' policy and he would have had no luck in defecting there.)

He has no license to practice medicine in Hong Kong. The medical exam to obtain a license is given in English. Joseph found himself a job as a messenger (about as good as he could get in an English-speaking colony) and begins to teach himself English. He soon discovers that he needs to work 16 hours a day to make enough money to survive. He decides to combine the two and find work where he can learn English. His decision leads him to apply for domestic work with any English-speaking family that will take him.

Allan and James decide to help him with English. This is the blind leading the blind. James' English is passable but Allan still speaks Spanish much of the time. Joseph soon realizes that he is never going to get anywhere speaking pidgin Spanish/English/ Chinese and hides in his room to study until the boys go to bed. Later in the evening he comes out and sits with me to study and ask questions. His ability to absorb a new language that bears no resemblance to Chinese is astounding.

Joseph has enjoyed high status and respect in China. Yet he has no qualms about working as a cook and housekeeper. He cheerfully cleans toilets, makes beds, and picks up after the boys without the slightest appearance of resentment at this change in status. As a housekeeper, he is tolerable after learning about the new machines - washing machines and dryers, etc.

As cook, Joseph is a disaster. He can boil rice badly and his other efforts are worse. I eventually take over most of the cooking. Some of his early efforts are memorable. He can follow recipes in English but has a tendency to modify them in strange ways.

I give him a recipe for meat loaf. He reads it and asks what type of meat should be used. I explain that usually ground beef is used, but that ground pork is acceptable. That evening, he serves us a gray, gelatinous mass that quivers when moved.

"What is this?"

"Meat roaf."

"Meat ro..loaf? What did you put in it?"

"I follow lecipe." He lists off all the correct ingredients. But something is not right.

"Where did you buy the ground beef?"

"I no buy. I make with beef in fleezer. I chop that." There is no beef in the freezer. I checked that morning and left him money to buy hamburger for this meal.

"Joseph, I looked this morning. There was no beef. Remember?"

"No, there is beef. I chop up river."

"River? Oh, you mean liv ... "

If you shut your eyes, meat loaf made with "glound river" isn't too bad. It certainly slides down easily.

There are other meals, too. Somehow, no matter how detailed the instructions, Joseph has a knack for following them precisely and screwing them up at the same time.

Frozen pizza is a favorite of the boys. Joseph is told it could be greatly improved by augmenting the topping with bits of meat or vegetables. Topped with whole broiled lettuce leaves, it not only takes on an interesting new appearance, but a unique taste.

Allan's delighted when I stumble across morcilla in the supermarket. Morcilla is a Spanish blood sausage. Allan explains to Joseph that the sausage makes wonderful sandwiches and asks for them in his school lunch for the next day. That evening, I find Allan glumly sitting in his room. Joseph has squeezed the uncooked blood from the sausages onto slices of bread and packed it in Allan's lunch. *"Father, it looked like a big scab."*

In spite of these disasters from the kitchen, we like Joseph very much and respect his initiative and desire to make a better life.

Joseph has a wife and two children still in Shanghai. To my surprise, telephoning Shanghai is easy and he often calls them. This did not seem to cause his family problems. Joseph asks for my help to obtain visas from the Hong Kong authorities for his family. This is, of course, impossible. Hong Kong has millions of Chinese with the same problem and the colonial government makes no exceptions.

One evening, after the boys go to bed, Joseph and I are discussing his family. He's a bit depressed about the seemingly indefinite separation. For no particular reason, I suggest that he see if his family can get into Macao. He sighs, and says, *"Government never approve. No relative in Macao."*

A few weeks later, I come home to a very excited and happy Joseph. His wife and children will arrive in Macao in two days! Joseph is convinced that I pulled strings with the Macao government for him. Actually, I have done nothing.

Macao had no I.I. problem. Its living conditions and economy are not much better than China and few Chinese want to escape to it. The Chinese Government believes the relative story and has issued exit visas for the family. The Macao authorities never bother to confirm the story and approve entry visas.

My involvement in Joseph's life becomes much more complicated at this point. Joseph has no travel documents and can not go to Macao. His family has no travel documents to travel from Macao to Hong Kong. I am often in Macao and now play Cupid.

Joseph asks me to help his wife settle and find employment. I ask if his wife has worked in China, since one of his children is only 5 years old.

"Yes, my wife is an opthamologist and an M.D." (By this time Joseph's English was very good.) *"She practices in the same hospital in Shanghai that I worked in."*

I go to Macao the day after his family arrives there. I have called Father Lancelot and ask him to arrange for us to meet in his office. My meeting with Joseph's wife is a real surprise.

She has brown hair, freckles, and looks like she is fresh from Bavaria. Her two kids, a boy aged 16 and the little girl, are typical Chinese kids. On later visits, she shows me pictures of her family. Her grandfather had, in fact, been a German brewer who came to China to build and run the Shanghai brewery that still produces beer. He remained there, married a Chinese, and produced a large family. In her family portraits, the group looks like a typical

Chinese family, except for one little German-looking girl in the middle. There is no explanation why only one of the many grandchildren looks like the grandfather.

She has a difficult life until she marries Joseph. The Chinese are not tolerant of foreigners and especially of mixed blood Chinese. She met Joseph in medical school and she often refers to the difficulties that his marriage made for him as well. I learn that this family was more exceptional than I thought.

Macao, being Portuguese, is not as rigid with medical licenses. Since she trained in western medicine, Father Lancelot immediately hires her for the refugee camp. She proves to be an excellent doctor.

I ask a British doctor friend about Joseph's chances for obtaining a license in Hong Kong to practice medicine.

"Nil, I suspect. The medical training system in China is poor and based upon oriental medicine. The colony is full of Chinese trained doctors and I don't know of one who is licensed. Hasn't got a chance, I'd say."

There are 2,200 medical schools in China. Four of them are exclusively for training in western medicine. Joseph and his wife have graduated from one of these schools. While we are on home leave, Joseph sits for the British medical exam, passes it without difficulty, and immediately begins to work in a Hong Kong Government hospital. He could have set up a private practice but believes that his service in a government hospital is the least that he can do in return for the opportunities that Hong Kong has made for him. He also obtains a document that allows him to travel to Macao and back. The Macao authorities allow him to stay for 24 hours once a month.

Over the years, I have lost track of Dr. Mei Ling Tak, his wife and children. They are survivors; I know that they have done well.

Work settled into a routine of refugee processing. It had regular hours. Hong Kong was a fascinating place to live and a great place for 2 teenage boys. It was safe, easy to traverse on bus lines and had lots to do. We rented Chinese junks for office gatherings and cruised to outer uninhabited islands for swimming and picnics. There were beaches everywhere. The boys and I could wander streets, markets, temples and many other activities. The school was outstanding and both boys began to catch up on all those years of missed education.

Unfortunately, things worsened with Anne Henshaw. She began to keep gin bottles in her desk and was often drunk before noon. She went from non-productive to counterproductive, arriving drunk at social events and business meetings with the UN and other countries. Finally I had no choice but to go back to the Consul General. Poor Anne clearly would not survive much longer unless something was done. I was surprised when Shoesmith declined to do anything and told me to deal directly with Washington about the situation.

I called Hank Cushing. His response was classic: *"She's a woman, she's a lawyer. No way will I take that on."* My last hope was the Embassy nurse. A tough British nurse, she had full authority in health issues. I explained the situation. She asked me to call her the next time Anne was in the office drunk. I walked across the street to our office and called the nurse only a few minutes after leaving her clinic. The nurse came right over, entered Anne's office, and closed the door. She was in there a long time. When she left, she said nothing to me.

About 15 minutes later Anne appeared with red eyes (nothing unusual) and tears. I braced myself for an enormous blowup. I didn't get it. To my astonishment, Anne more or less said the following: *"I know I have a problem. I know it is out of control. I am too proud to ask for help and nobody every seemed to care. Thank you."*

Well now, that was not the reaction I expected! With it out in the open, or so she thought, since the whole Consulate already knew, Anne tried the local alcoholic treatment experts. It didn't help and I must have had the nurse over every day for the next week. Anne did not want to go back to the States for treatment and Shoesmith – the only person who could have ordered it – still thought it was my problem. That attitude ended on the 4th of July.

As is the custom of every American Embassy in the world, on the 4th of July a reception is held and all the other embassies are invited. The large reception room of the Consulate was on the 4th floor. It was a weekend and I was the Duty Officer. The weekend Duty Officer duties rotate among all the officers and it usually only took about one weekend a year. This weekend was my turn. I sat in the Consul General's outer office facing the elevator. A formally dressed Marine greeted guests at the door of the Consulate and escorted them to the elevator. As the elevator door opened, a second Marine pointed out the reception room.

The elevator door opens and Anne emerges, hair a tangled mess and lipstick more or less in the general area of her mouth. As she staggered her way down the hallway, the Marine turned to me, clicked his heels, gave a snappy salute, and said, *"Sir! Miss Henshaw is shit-faced!"* It was sad but it was funny.

A few moments later, The Admin. Officer came down the hallway, propelling Anne in front of him, and disappeared into the elevator. Finally, my problem – as Shoesmith put it – was now our problem. Anne was gone in a week.

[Anne's "thanks" to me was genuine. She went back to the States and entered a rehab center, dried out and seemed to be getting on with her life. She married a retired Foreign Service

Officer and seemed very happy. Her husband suddenly died on a tennis court. She kept in contact but about a year later I learned that she had killed herself, leaving behind a note that she 'couldn't cope with it any longer.']

Anne's replacement was Jere Brokhan. He was a nice person but another with no Vietnam experience or language. He did, however, run the office very well so that I could now spend almost all of my time in the refugee camps selecting and interviewing. We were soon moving 2,500 refugees a month to the States.

My interviews weeded out the North Vietnamese. When the communists first started to expel the dissidents and Chinese, they considered it a punishment. However, soon letters came into Vietnam from resettled refugees living in California, France and other places, with stories of financial success and better standards of living, as well as educational opportunities for their children. Soon many northern Vietnamese were also leaving to join the boat people. They had no claims to refugee status and few countries would take them.

In terms of intelligence from Vietnam it was clear that the country had its hands full with reconstruction and consolidation. Much of what I learned was interesting and reportable but of little use. The search for MIAs and POWs did produce information that leads to the return of American dead. By 1980 the Vietnamese government wanted foreign assistance and world acceptance and did, in fact, cooperate and assist in the location of our dead.

I located 221 MIAs in a single interview. A toady little man claimed that he was the 'official mortician' for the Vietnamese government. For a large sum of money and quick resettlement in the US, he offered to give me information about the location where the Vietnamese government stored the remains of recovered American dead and POWs that died in captivity.

My counter-offer involved him avoiding some very unpleasant and very uncomfortable experiences after I turned him over to some very nasty people. (I didn't actually know any 'very nasty people' but he didn't know that.) I gave him about 2 minutes to decide. I added that if he was lying to me he probably would regret doing so. He cooperated but said that he feared for his life if he was identified as the source. I frankly did not completely believe his story and claims but he did have some details that would have been difficult to fabricate.

In the last 24 hours of our Embassy presence in Saigon, 2 Marine guards were killed by a rocket that hit the building. We were unable to get their bodies out of the country in those last hours. He claimed that the bodies were shipped to him in Hanoi where he dismembered them, boiled the parts, and boxed and labeled the bones. He claimed that this was the procedure with American POWs who died in captivity and all American bodies found by the North Vietnamese. He said that they were stored in an old movie theater in Hanoi. My conclusion was that he was either telling the truth or a raving lunatic. I passed the information on and, within 36 hours, a US agent in Hanoi confirmed that the claimed theater was filled with boxes. While the North Vietnamese were cooperating, at this point, in locating American remains at crash sites and battlefields, apparently they decided that keeping a little 'insurance' for the future would be a good idea.

The 'mortician' left Hong Kong on a special military plane. Our government was able to confirm the important parts of his claims and the North Vietnamese quietly returned the remains. The man's fear of retaliation was not unlikely and today he lives in the US under the Witness Protection Program.

I also covered the refugees in nearby Macau. The camps there are run by the Catholic Church through Father Lancelot Rodriques. Lancelot was a tall man, a mixture of British, Malay and various other things. Born in Malacca, he was shipped off at age 11 to Macau in 1939 for schooling, just in time for the war. Cut off from his family and kept alive by the church, at the end of the war the now 17 year old joined the Jesuits and stayed on. He was a true character, a bit difficult to take at first but a truly good person at heart. He drank like a fish, sang loudly in restaurants, shamelessly shook down the casino owners for money and did a great deal of good in the Portuguese colony.

My first meeting with Lancelot was unique, to say the least. The phone system between Macau and Hong Kong ran through China and worked sporadically. My secretary finally reached him and made the arrangements for me to make my first visit. He was to meet me at the ferry. I was concerned that we might not recognize each other. The staff all agreed – we would recognize each other.

I came off the ferry to see one head above all the others. I was the only non-Chinese on the boat. Lancelot approached through the crowd and said, *"Why, in God's name, did you come so early?"* It was 8 o'clock.

"This is the normal hour I start work."

"Follow me."

At the door, illegally parked, Lancelot's car and driver sat. We climbed in and drove about 100 yards and parked, again illegally, in front of his office.

Lancelot shared his small office with Father ***** who ran the Vatican spy network in the People's Republic. (A quite effective system, I might add.) He disappeared, as he would do anytime I showed up.

Now seated, Lancelot opened our day with, *"Scotch or coffee?"* Thinking that he could not be serious, I laughed and asked for coffee. Lancelot disappeared down the hallway and returned with a rattling cup on a small tray. I took the coffee while he reached into a desk drawer, pulled out a bottle of Johnny Walker Black Label and poured himself about three fingers worth in a water glass. A few sips and he seemed much more ready to begin his day.

We toured the three refugee camps. The residents were crowded but receiving good care. Later in the day, I began to interview some of the refugees pre-screened by the staff. It quickly became obvious that the refugees in Macau were in general less educated and, well, to be frank, less intelligent than those in Hong Kong. It took awhile to figure this out.

Coming from Vietnam, boats first pass Macau. Most of the boat people looked at tiny Macau, with its few multi storied buildings, and continued on. The less educated or those who did not deduce what they were seeing thought they had reached Hong Kong and stopped.

Usually at the end of my day, I would meet Lancelot for dinner at some restaurant. I never got a bill. I pointed out to him that the US government paid my bills and that it was illegal for me to accept his payment for my expenses. Lancleot laughed, *"Good Heavens, you don't think I pay for this, do you? I have so much 'dirt' on most of these restaurant owners that they wouldn't dare give me a bill."* If I stayed over for the night, the same thing happened with the hotel bill.

For all his good intentions, Lancelot continually caused me problems. The high speed ferries stopped running at sundown. Unable to pick up the many wooden fishing boats on radar, they could not operate safely in the dark. On numerous occasions I would be at dinner with Lancelot when the hour to leave approached. Getting away from him was impossible. He would just call the ferry company and tell them to not depart until I arrived 15 or 30 minutes late. Then I had to face several hundred angry passengers when I climbed aboard.

When he discovered that I had two boys, he invited all of us for a weekend during the school holidays. We went over on a Friday. While I interviewed refugees in the camp, he offered to show the boys around Macau and meet us at a certain restaurant. When I walked in, both boys had a large beer in front of them. Simultaneously, they both pointed at Lancelot, *"He did it!!"* I was hardly concerned since both boys could not stand even the odor of alcohol.

On another weekend visit, he took me to lunch where, in spite of my best efforts, he managed to get me three sheets to the wind. While not drunk, I was close. We – well, I – reeled out of the restaurant and into his car. I thought we were headed for the ferry until his driver pulled up to some large steel gates and honked the horn. The gates opened and we pulled into the middle of a soccer field with a large crowd of screaming and cheering high school students. The car stops in front of a microphone stand. I slink down in my seat as Lancelot gets out of the car, approaches the mike and announces that the American Consul has arrived to hand out the awards for some sports competition between the several high schools in Macau. The local press is waiting.

With no chance of escape, I climbed out of the car and walked in a more or less straight line to the traditional Olympic-style three tiered boxes for the prize winners to stand upon. The awards are medals on ribbons to be placed over the heads of the winners. While trying to look sober, I placed the ribbons over the first three which caused a great deal of laughter from the crowd. Oddly they had the prize winners facing me instead of the crowd. The boxes were marked 2,1,3 with the traditional first place winner on a box slightly higher than the other two. However, the boxes on the crowd side were reversed – 3,1,2. I was giving the second and third place medals to the wrong persons. Somebody whispered in my ear and I got the rest correctly placed. I dreaded how this would all be in the next day's paper. Finally finished I wove my way back to the still parked car and a hugely amused Lancelot.

Then Lancelot began a new campaign. By this time Lancelot knows Allan and James well enough to decide that they are reasonably happy and well-adjusted boys. In the beginning, he jokingly tells me that I need more kids. Later he more seriously suggests that I consider adopting another child in Macau. At first I don't give this a lot of thought. My hands are full enough, it seems. But Lancelot has planted a seed and I do begin to think about it more often. I mention the idea to Allan and James. Allan doesn't have much reaction to the idea, perhaps because he does not think I am serious. James plainly does not like the idea. In a few months I do begin to give this idea real consideration. The boys and I have more discussions about this. Allan thinks it is OK - James doesn't like the idea at all.

The state of Virginia has changed its laws for single adopting parents. Previously, only same sex adoptions were legal and the limit of two international adoptions is no longer in effect with I.N.S. In early 1980, I decide to look for a little sister for Allan and James.

On a regular visit to Macau, I ask Lancelot about the Macanese adoption system. With a broad smile, he picks up the phone and makes a call. *"Wait a few minutes and I'll have the expert here,"* he says.

Shortly a quite fat nun comes puffing into his office. Father Lancelot introduces me to Sister Lillian Cayer, a French-Canadian nun. She's lived in China for years until the

Communist government throws out the Catholic missionaries. She has moved to Macau and now operates a day care center and arranges a few adoptions when she can. Foreign adoptions in Macau are infrequent. She mumbles incessantly, mostly to herself, in a mixture of English, French, and Chinese. I explain our family history to her and she is delighted.

On my next visit, she has arranged a meeting for me. The first child she introduces to me is a beautiful little girl about 4 years old. James comes with me to see her and thinks the little girl is terrific! However, when I actually agree to pursue an adoption, the little girl's sister (and only remaining family member) changes her mind and will not release the little girl for adoption.

Sister Lillian calls me about a week later to look at an 8-year-old child who possessed both male and female sex organs. I told her I was not interested. My health insurance would not cover this anyway. *"You should come and look! It's really interesting,"* she said. No thought about the child's feelings. I decline to take the zoo tour.

A few weeks later, Sister Lillian calls me in Hong Kong (still not easy in those days) and asks me to come look at a little boy. James and I make an appointment and make a special trip to Macau. We go to a building near the Chinese border and wait in the drawing room of the nun's quarters. Sister Lillian spends a few minutes serving tea and telling me all the virtues of the boy about to be presented. A tall Chinese woman comes into the room with a very small boy dressed in a dirty T-shirt, dirty shorts, and worn flip-flops. The kid matches the clothes - no front teeth at all, a head covered with fuzz after being recently shaved for lice, and smelling very badly. Sister Lillian explains, *"The boy stays in a school during the week. The boy's mother picked him up there to come to this appointment. She brought just as she found him in at the school."* Some school.

The little boy is very passive. He stands quietly beside his mother's chair until told to sit down. He shows little interest in us or his surroundings, unafraid, bored if anything. His mother says almost nothing and does not look at me. Sister Lillian extols the boy's virtues as if he's a used car. *"Just a little washing and good as new! And we will throw in a spare."* (Not exactly like this, but almost. Sister Lillian had her heart in the right place but wasn't the most sensitive person.) She tells us this little boy also has a brother up for adoption.

I'm not very comfortable with this meeting. I had not expected a mother. In fact, I had assumed that any child we saw would have no parents. Sister Lillian does know U.S. Immigration law, however, and knows that a child with one living parent is adoptable. She explains that the boy's father has died.

"I'm sympathetic but really don't want TWO more children."

It would be very bad to split them up. Besides, you can't buy one shoe, can you?" This was one of the most appalling comments I've heard over the years, rivaling the offer to line up the kids in Ibague for adoption inspection. With Sister Lillian ignoring this type of comment is about the only thing to be done. She clearly thought she had a live customer in me.

Half joking, I say, *"There can't possibly be two children in Macau this unattractive and dirty."*

Lillian stands up, goes to the door, and returns with an absolutely matching kid - smell and all.

She stands the identical twin boys side by side. As they stand there, holding each other's hands and studiously examining their toes, I am becoming intrigued. They really are just two little boys at a particularly unattractive time of childhood. The dirt will come off. They are also the first (and only) Chinese identical twins that I've ever seen.

Thirteen year old James is NOT impressed. He begins to give me reasons why we should perhaps hold out a little longer and look at some other kids. I think he saw the look on my face and realized he might just get two brothers in this deal.

"How can I explain two Chinese brothers?" he says.

"You've done alright explaining me. Tell people they're adopted. What were you expecting in China? Blondes? It's not exactly as if this will suddenly make our family look strange. Shall we hold out for a Chinese kid that looks like you? Or me?"

Actually that is a cheap shot and James does have a point. Most people assume that I have (or had) a dark wife. Since we left Colombia, few people pay much notice to the boys and me. James thinks over the possibility of telling people that this possible new brother is adopted and seems satisfied with the explanation of Chinese brothers.

"But look at them - who knows what they will look like when they get older. Maybe they will stay this ugly!" Hmmm, maybe he does have another point. I certainly would not choose children because of looks but, let's face it, when you have a choice why not consider it as one of the factors. James and Allan were among the better looking kids in Ibague. While I agree that this might be a concern, I'm not ready to just say no. James suggests that perhaps the twins have an older brother to look at so we might get an idea of what the future held. Sister Lillian, who is listening carefully to our conversation, tells us that the twins have an older brother waiting outside.

Sister Lillian again goes through the door. She returns in a few minutes with the twins' brother, Che Kam Pang. The brother, who is 15, says little but makes it clear that he doesn't like his brothers being adopted, he doesn't like James or me, he doesn't like this meeting, and he doesn't like the whole idea. Inscrutable is not this boy's strong point. Nonetheless, Pang is a nice looking young man and one could see SOME resemblance between brothers. James and I leave without making a commitment. Lillian is, of course, hot to trot off to court now.

Back in Hong Kong, Allan, James, and I discuss it. James speaks eloquently and, unfortunately, very accurately about what he observed. Allan, in spite of the descriptions, says he thinks it a good idea. This is a slight change from his earlier comment that I would do what I wanted anyway. True enough, but I do want to know their attitude and will not proceed if they both really don't like the idea. James talks himself into living with it, especially after I comment that he might like to be a big brother for a change.

This time I don't have the serious doubts that I had with Allan and James. I've been a single father now for five years and am confident that I can increase our family and handle it. Well, handle it to the extent that I ever do. I can't love Allan and James any more than I do now. My life has improved so incredibly with two fantastic sons. I have a wonderful family and want to include two more boys. I hope that perhaps these two little boys can expand our home and become a part of what is the most important thing in life for me. No doubts this time.

Father Lancelot advises me to hire a lawyer. He introduces me to an old Portuguese lawyer who speaks English. The lawyer advises me that he knows of no single person adopting a child in Macau. He isn't sure it is legal. The law states that husband and wife must both agree to any adoptions. It is not clear that a person must be married. Here we go again! I tell him, inaccurately and, yes, dishonestly, that the laws of Colombia were the same and the Colombians decided it was legal. He asks if I have a copy of the law in Colombia. I give him a copy of the law in Colombia before it was changed. (Portuguese and Spanish as so similar that it is easy to read one if you speak the other.) I "forget" to tell him that the Colombian law was modified to allow single parent adoptions. On my behalf, the lawyer consults with the judge. They decide that if I am OK with Colombia, well, then I am OK with Portugal.

Sister Lillian is not the most honest person and thinks that little lies to help people are all right with God. She does not worry much about the law. She wants me to take them back to Hong Kong on some pretext until the adoption is approved in the courts. This, of course, is illegal in Macau, in Hong Kong and in the United States, but doesn't bother her a bit. I refuse. The issue of this adoption not being approved remains and I am not about to take two kids home, only to return them later. We do decide to put them into an English language school while I wait. I will pick up the bills. They will live at the school just as they are now doing and go home every other weekend. I thought it odd, and still do, that their mother never placed any of the other kids in a boarding school. Throughout the whole process, I watch Sister Lillian carefully. She constantly embellishes facts on documents to make them look better even when it serves no real purpose.

About a month later, I take Allan and James, along with Spencer, a Chinese friend, back to Macau to work on the adoption papers with the lawyer, introduce the twins to their future brothers, and to get as much information about their background as possible. I especially want as much as possible about their medical history. We go to Henry's, a restaurant on the sidewalk of the Pria Grande, next to the harbor, to have lunch with the twins, their mother, and Sister Lillian. I brought Spencer because I distrust any translation from Lillian, knowing that she is inclined to say whatever she thinks best. Their brother, Pang, and sister also come. While we talk, through Spencer, the twins eat watermelon and end up looking like the first time I saw them. At least this time, they start out clean and odorless. Pang decides that I'm not so bad after all and begins to warm up to me. If you call occasionally raising his eyes to glance at me "warming up." At least his glances are not so hostile this time.

Actually, I take this hostility as a good sign.

Pang really cares for his brothers and does not want to see them go. He must love them and want to protect them.

The twins are somewhat more animated this time but still sit quietly most of the time. Their brothers and sister are much more active. They say little and do not seem interested in more than lunch.

After lunch is finished at the restaurant we go to the twins' house. The house is behind the race track stand near the Macau-Hong Kong ferry landing. It has two rooms constructed of wooden frames covered with corrugated aluminum sheets for the roof and walls. The living half has a dirt floor, a raised earthen platform for the eight of them to sleep on, a small refrigerator and TV from more prosperous days, and a single water tap out front. The other half is concrete pigpens. The whole house is about ten feet wide and thirty feet long. While we are talking, Fu wanders outside, drops his shorts and pees on the water tap. (I was beginning to be able to tell them apart.).

I have a Polaroid camera and took some pictures of the family. In an effort to reduce the still obvious hostility from brother Pang, I show him how to operate my Polaroid. Pang takes pictures of us, which I give him.

In late June, 1980, I go to the court in Macau with Father Lancelot as my translator. The judge speaks English quite well but the language used in the court must be Portuguese. We met in the judge's office. It's informal and the judge is a very nice person. After a few required questions, the adoption is approved. The ferry does not arrive in Hong Kong until after midnight. The boys have not dozed off at all on the ferry. Immigration takes longer than usual because of the special papers I have for the twins. The Chinese Immigration officer, usually friendly, tonight is formal with us. We take a taxi back to the apartment on the other side of the island. The twins are still wide-awake and excited by Hong Kong. Unlike Hong Kong,

 Macau is almost flat. The taxi chugs up the high mountain of Hong Kong Island, giving the boys a good view of the panorama of the city. They are excited and babbling away with the driver. From the look of the taxi driver, I suspect they are giving him a version of today's events. I have no idea what is being said but it is clear that they were only the quite, solemn little boys when around their mother.

Two weeks later the three of us return to Macau for the final court appearance. The judge doesn't really ask such. He calls the two boys into the room. They come bouncing into the courtroom, dressed in nice clothes, and the judge asks them in Chinese, *"Who is your father?"* They both grin broadly and point at me. He signs some papers and it is done. I discover that Lillian has named them David Che Kam Fu Kassebaum and Andrew Che Kam Hap Kassebaum. Quite the monikers for such small boys.

The twins begin their new lives in Hong Kong as David and Andrew. Sister Lillian has taught them their names. These are the only English words they recognize when we depart for Hong Kong. A few days later, Lillian comes to visit - and to tell me that she taught them the wrong names. So Andrew becomes David and vice-versa. This confuses all of us for a few days.

Our doctor-cook Joseph is the single language bridge to the twins for month between the twins' arrival in Hong Kong and our departure for the United States for vacation. Joseph does not understand why I would adopt the twins. Actually he doesn't understand why I would adopt anybody. He likes Allan and James but we were a unit when he came. I suspect he does not like the idea of Chinese raised as Americans. Still, Joseph made a big difference in the way our relationship with the twins began. He was quiet and gentle with them. They would sit and talk with him for hours in the evenings.

Meanwhile the refugee program became more and more chaotic. With representatives from over ten countries now interviewing in the camps, we began to step on each other's toes. Some refugees would get interviewed and accepted by several countries and then pick and choose their destination. This resulted in much wasted effort. All attempts to get the United Nations to place a system to prevent this were ignored or, as the United Nations Representative told me, *"We are not an operational agency."* He drove around in his big car with a driver, gave press conferences, and attended or gave a lot of cocktail parties.

Tired of wasting my time interviewing refugee families that then went to France or Canada or wherever, I asked the representatives of all the other countries to meet with me. We met and I proposed that we collectively tell the UN that we would not interview one more refugee until they established a system to see that the refugees were referred to us consecutively. To my somewhat surprise, they all agreed and the British were delegated to relay the message to the UN along with an implied threat to notify to press that the flow of refugees would stop until the UN acted. I later learned that the British also informed the UN Rep. that, lacking any action, Her Majesty's Government saw no reason for the UN office to remain in the colony. They had one month to set up a system.

The UN Rep. and staff were too useless to act but, backed into a corner, hired a staff and brought in a young Indian woman named Terry to set up a system. The system consisted of taking a copy of the British camp residents file and referring them to one country at a time. After the first country accepted the refugees for resettlement, they were not interviewed by any other country. Not exactly rocket science but even this system took the UN a month to implement.

Terry proved to be sharp and hard working. Soon the UN system referred the refugees first to the countries that might most readily accept them.

Terry and I went out quite a few times, including the annual Marine Ball. After awhile it was clear that she had many plans for her future that did not include 4 kids. We drifted apart amicably.

While the twins fall easily into the roles of my sons and brothers to Allan and James, there is a small undercurrent in Hong Kong of hostility toward our family. Chinese in Hong Kong cannot be adopted by "foreign devils." The British did not generally intermarry with the Chinese. The Chinese rarely intermarry with non-Chinese. Although I knew hundreds, if not thousands, of people in Hong Kong, I knew of no local interracially married or adopted families. (Well, one, actually – An Australian-Chinese, born and raised in Australia, married to an Australian woman. He was later posted to Hong Kong and they had twin sons in the American school.) My large Chinese staff of now about 90 fell into three groups. The largest group did not like this adoption (but were smart enough to say nothing); another group ignored it; and a small group took it as a strange exception to a good rule. Their view of Allan and James and I was neutral. Foreign devils with foreign devils, I suppose.

After more than three years in Hong Kong, Hank Cushing calls me on the phone from Washington. He asks if, in my opinion, we could consider closing down the refugee office in Hong Kong. By this time, the flow of refugees from Vietnam had dwindled into a trickle. By 1982 we had interviewed and approved almost all of the refugees that the United States would take, and the Consulate was capable of dealing with the small number of refugees that would appear in the future. The contract staff in my office could handle the remaining work without a full-time State Department officer. With reluctance, since this was the nicest post of my career, I told Hank that I did believe that the office could close. Jere Brokhan was on leave at the time and I don't think he ever forgave me.

The Philippines

We arrived in Manila when Allan was in grade 11, James in grade 9 and the twins in the second grade. They were all doing well in school, mostly caught up, and able to deal with English without problems. The twins only spoke English by this time, albeit with a strong Chinese accent that they would lose in another few years. While in Hong Kong, Allan and James had discovered that girls were not just soft boys. Allan liked them all, James seemed to have one at a time.

The Embassy had asked if they could do anything to assist the move and I had requested that they find me a housekeeper that could and would control two teenage boys and two rambunctious 9 year olds. This request might sound easy but it is often the case that household help spoils and indulges the children. We arrived to find 'Tita.' Tita was barely taller than the twins and I had my doubts. She filled the bill perfectly, however, and had no problem backing one of the boys up against the wall and shaking her finger at them. I did not have to worry when I was not home. They were all good kids but I did not want temptations while I was gone.

Not home was a problem. One camp was in Bataan, the other on the distant island of Palawan. Bataan terrified me as the Embassy drivers went 80 or 90 mph over bad roads littered with kids, cows and potholes. I could get there and back in one terrifying day. Bataan had a large population of refugees but most of them had been approved in other places and transferred to this camp for a few months of intensive orientation and language before moving on to be resettled in the States. A few boat people did reach the Philippines directly and needed to be interviewed but my visits were infrequent.

Palawan was a short plane ride but required a stay of several days in order to not waste the taxpayer's money on travel needlessly. This camp population was boat people who arrived directly from Vietnam. On my first trip out to Palawan, I was met and guided about by Hazel McIntyre, a United Nations volunteer who did the psychological assessments of refugee suffering the traumas of the trip across the ocean. She seemed to know everybody and took me from place to place introducing me to dozens of people, most of whom I could not place on the next trip.

Over the next few months each time I came out to Palawan Hazel and I would have lunch and/or dinner together, always in a group.

At age 38 I had quit looking for a marriage partner. Over the years of fatherhood I met numerous women, many of who were interested in me or my position or my income. I liked a lot of them but there always was some problem. I usually waited awhile before they saw my children. Some women were put off by the number and ages of my sons, some feigned interest but I could see through it immediately. Some wanted visas and others what they saw as a more comfortable life.

On distant Palawan, Hazel knew about my family but had no opportunity to meet them. A few months after we first met, Hazel was in Manila for some reason and we met by chance at a boring Embassy cocktail party. I had already promised the boys to take them to Pagasanjan Falls the next day. I invited Hazel to come along – rather foolish in my small Mazda. She agreed.

The Falls were a long drive and not very comfortable. One twin sat on Hazel's lap while the other drew the luggage space behind the rear seat. It rained and we ended up eating a picnic lunch in a bus stop shelter full of goat turds. Hazel seemed to be having a great time.

At the Falls we hired two canoes and split up for the long paddle up to the Falls. I always felt guilty about this part of the trip since the canoes were paddled by two skinny Filipino kids. At the top and Falls we all swam for awhile and enjoyed the scenery. The trip back is very fast as the canoes shot through the rapids that were so much work coming up.

In the afternoon we headed back to Manila and, unusual for me, I got hopelessly lost. Instead of arriving home for dinner it was more like midnight before we found out way back. Through all of this Hazel still seemed to be having a good time.

When you find the right person you just KNOW. On this more or less disastrous outing I KNEW. Here finally was a person who enjoyed travel, didn't mind the occasional discomforts that come with travel, liked my kids and was fun to be with. She was the first women I knew that I felt would be just as desirable 10 or 20 years later.

Over the next few weeks I spent a lot of time in Palawan and not just to process refugees. As New Year's Eve approached I invited Hazel to spend the evening with me.

I sat down with Allan and James and told them that I hoped to propose to Hazel on New Year's Eve. James thought it was terrific, Allan did not object but was a bit more reserved about it.

The twins were too young to be consulted at this point.

On the 31st of December Hazel arrived to change her clothes at the house before we went out for the evening. I had bought an engagement ring.

I asked," *Will you marry me?*" She looked surprised. She thought for a few minutes as I sweated.

"Maybe."

"Maybe! That's not an answer!" (This could turn out to be a really uncomfortable New Year's Eve.)

"Yes."

We talked awhile before coming out of the bedroom. As we reached the top of the stairway we saw Allan and James at the bottom.

"What did she say?"

I think Hazel felt a bit ganged upon at that point.

We were married less than six weeks later.

As soon as we were married, she left me. With a few months left on her contract with the United Nations, she had to return to

Palawan. I spent an inordinate amount of time there with no complaints from the office.

Once her contract was completed, Hazel moved to Manila and we began a true married life. For me and the boys, it was an easy transition with a few accommodations to be made. The boys were comfortable walking around the house in various states of undress but quit doing so when asked. For awhile, the two older boys were not sure what to call Hazel and so it was along the lines of *"Hey"* until *"Mom"* felt comfortable.

We stayed on in Manila for a few more months but the Refugee Program was winding down and I was frankly getting tired of the daily stories of drama, death, starvation, and political repression. I finally asked to be relieved and to return to the States.

I returned a second time to U.S.A.I.D. in Washington. It was boring and uninteresting but I did want a time for us to settle down into a somewhat normal life and for the two older boys to graduate from an American school. I stuck it out for more than 4 years. By this time U.S.A.I.D. had been reduced to barely more than a contracting agency funneling money to well-connected companies and agencies that did a desultory job of foreign aid. I pushed paper and came close to dying of boredom.

CHAD

By 1989 Allan was in college and James accepted for his first year of university. The twins would not head off to university for another 6 years. I could not stand the boredom any longer and began to seek an overseas post. CORDS was long gone, the State Department Refugee Program gone and my background did not fit well into the current programs of any branch of the Foreign Service. In a time of relative peace, the Foreign Service had attracted a certain type of individual and had settled into a rather comfortable time of routine activities in diplomacy, foreign aid and political reporting. Nonetheless there remained a series of Embassies in 'less desirable' countries that held little attraction for most FSOs. This included many African countries and the Middle East. When offered a post in Chad, I jumped at it.

Chad, Ethiopia, and Vietnam competed yearly for the title of "Poorest Country on Earth." Chad usually won. Landlocked, mostly Sahara desert, lacking in natural resources and dumped by the French colonists with little infrastructure, educated people trained government people, Chad had been governed by a series of petty dictators who stole as much as possible before being run out of the country by the successor dictator. The Chadian

Government ceased to exist a few miles outside of the capital and meant little to the average Chadian. Only a handful of countries even bothered to maintain an Embassy in the country – the USA, France, Germany, neighboring Sudan, Egypt and China.

The American Embassy had only three FSOs, a Military Attache, and a few others in communications and intelligence. The A.I.D. office generally had about 8 FSOs to run a small program. Actual foreign aid equaled less money than the operating costs of the office. This portion of the program operated small program in health, education, agriculture, road building and accounting. The largest portion of A.I.D.'s budget consisted of funding for the Chadian military. While not exactly secret, this military funding went unnoticed by the distant American press and we were expected to keep it that way. (The annual budget generally was in the neighborhood of $7.5 million. Of this $2.5 million funded foreign aid with $5 million for military assistance.) The French had a military contingent in Chad and thought that they had the upper hand with the Chadian military. However money talks and the Chadians came to us first.

When the Chadians overran a long established Libyan military base in northern Chad, the base was full of the latest Russian military weapons and equipment. The Chadians told us first and we quietly became the highest bidder. Under the pretext of an

A.I.D. foreign aid shipment – we had them regularly – a US Air Force C5A, the world's largest cargo plane, landed in the middle of the night, unloaded a heavy lift helicopter that flew north. It picked up the newest Russian equipment on several trips. It was loaded on the plane, along with the helicopter, and headed for the USA before the sum rose. The French were furious.

The rationale for this military program relied upon the long animosity between Libya and the United States and justified by the Libyan occupation of the northern part of Chad. Chad naturally wanted its territory back and the United States enjoyed keeping the Libyans occupied with the low level conflict that reduced its efforts to fund terrorists.

For six of the 24 months I was in Chad, I was the Mission Director (Acting) for one reason or another. As the Deputy Mission Director of AID I should not have been the direct manager of any project. Perhaps because of my background, I was handed the military program and was the only AID person involved in it. The funds paid salaries, supplied equipment and operated the Chadian Air Force – one old transport plane!

The French considered Chad to be their sphere of influence, based upon their years of badly managed colonialism. They resented our military program and this resentment almost immediately became directed at me, as the manager of the funds. While I had frequent meetings with the other embassies in Chad, I never met or worked with any French Embassy officials. The French did not seem to recognize that the Chadian government desperately needed funds for its Army and that our funding had influence. We also developed a network of Chadian friends.

Chad turned out to be a very enjoyable post for Hazel and me. We enjoyed most of the Americans in the Embassy and had frequent social contacts with the other embassies – except the French, of course. Our house was primitive but comfortable. It was large but poorly constructed of concrete blocks, a tin roof and a wooden ceiling made of old shipping pallets. The enormous living room, perhaps 50 feet square, had one electrical outlet. It was air conditioned but often required the operation of our noisy standby generator.

It was less pleasant for David and Andrew. There were few teenagers near their age that spoke any English and there were few facilities where they could go on their own. The school had only three kids in their class – and they were two of them. The second year Andrew wanted to go to boarding school and spent his grade 7 in Austria. The school there did not produce much in the way of quality education. As a result, Hazel and I did not extend for a second two year tour, although we would have done so gladly.

PERU

I transferred directly to Peru. After Chad, the city of Lima was urbane and its center both historic and attractive. The city had hundreds of parks and were well tended. There were restaurants and other diversions of world-class quality. While the city was surrounded by slums inhabited by very poor and desperate people, this was not apparent at first. The crime rate was high and the country had a problem with a revolutionary group, the Sendero Luminosa or Shining Path. Crime was high. The revolutionaries targeted government installations and generally were not a problem to the rest of the population. This would change.

Peru would prove to be the most miserable and unpleasant tour of my career. Fortunately it was at the end and I had little to lose by expressing myself. That I did and made few friends in the process.

The Peru program totaled about $180 million a year. About $5 million went to development aid and $175 million for an ill-fated, ineffective politically motivated anti-narcotics program. In addition the Mission was full of corrupt American and Peruvian employees.

This was one of those 'find your own housing' posts. The only recommended realtor was the brother of the Peruvian wife of the Controller – the man who paid the rent. The entire security contract belonged to the wife of another American employee who managed the payments to the company. His 'owner' wife delegated contract negotiations to her husband – the man who paid the bills! When I reported all of this to the Inspector General for investigation, they never showed up.

The small development portion of the program was two years behind in paying contractors and the entire program at a standstill. The Controller, responsible for making these payments, was fired for incompetence. A few years later he managed to get rehired. Meanwhile the few actual development programs either were at a complete standstill or closing down for lack of money. Few contractors were willing to spend their own money under these circumstances and the Peruvians simply did not have any money.

The anti-narcotics program had both a visible and invisible series of activities. The US Army had several bases hidden in the jungles of the Upper Huaga Valley. Controlled from Panama, their mission was to train and support the Peruvian Army in anti-narcotics missions and to supply arms and equipment to them. The Peruvians, of course, wanted the funds and equipment and so tolerated to the troops on the condition that they never leave their bases. On a visit to the area I toured one base where you could reach through the fence and pluck cocaine leaves. Our troops could do nothing. We later received photos of US supplied helicopters, manned by Peruvian troops, loading and delivering cocaine for the drug lords.

I wrote numerous reports and telegrams pointing out the absurdity of the military program. I finally received a phone call from Washington telling me, "You may be absolutely right but do not send any more of these reports." The program was politically driven. No Congressman would be willing to place US troops into drug saturated slums of, say, Washington, DC, or New York City but felt that they did need to demonstrate that they were doing something about the problem. Thus they could say that they supported the financing of this huge military program to fight drugs at the source.

The overt anti-narcotics program was actually more absurd. The idea was to train cocaine growers to grow vegetables, rather than cocaine, and sell them. This not only did not work but could not work. The cocaine areas are not connected by road to any other part of Peru. Short of airlifting vegetables to Lima there was no market for the produce. In addition, most cocaine growers were not even farmers. They were people from the cities who went into the jungle, cleared by burning off the area and then planted cocaine. Cocaine is a weed – it needs no care. These 'farmers' would plant and then return to the cities to wait until harvest time. Most had other jobs. These 'farmers', working for a week to plant and a week to harvest could make $15-$20 thousand dollars every six months. An acre of carrots might earn $100 after constant care, assuming they ever did get to a market. Nothing I could say or write could stop these programs.

I finally flew over the area in a helicopter. They cocaine growers, with nothing to fear from our troops, did not even look up as we passed over at treetop level. The area of cocaine under cultivation went as far as the horizon even at high altitude. Large volumes of chemicals used to process the drug were dumped into the river. All the fish were now dead and this river eventually drained into the Amazon River. It was and is a serious problem.

Our house was, well, magnificent. Five bedrooms, three dining rooms, three living rooms, a library, a music room, a weight room and sauna and a large pool. The guest quarters were located over the six car garage and larger than our house in Washington. The school for the twins was also beautifully built and equipped. It was, however, surrounded by a 20 foot wall with armed guards in bunkers at the corners. Allan and James were now in college and not with us.

Life outside the office was quite pleasant. We traveled about the coast and spent many evenings in Lima's restaurants and clubs. Unfortunately, after about six months the Sendero Luminoso changed tactics. They stopped concentrating on government facilities and began to place small bombs randomly around the city in trash cans or doorways to businesses closed for the evening. The explosions killed randomly and the city's vibrant nightlife simply disappeared. The formerly busy areas were deserted by 7 o'clock in the evening.

The final straw came at the twin's school. At the front gate there was a pay phone used by the students. It was found to be rigged with a grenade. Fortunately no students were injured but it did trigger an evacuation of dependants back to the States. I moved from the large house to an apartment that could only be entered by a keyed elevator. Our office was hit by a bazooka and it blew out all my office windows. I had stepped out for a moment.

I spent the rest of the tour approving expenditures for good development projects that never were paid and millions of dollars for a failed antinarcotics program – that were paid. I was happy to leave Peru and return to family and Washington.

With only a few years left until eligible for retirement I looked back at my eight overseas tours. Of these only three were with AID and only one – Chad – had provided much personal or professional satisfaction. I did what I seemed to do best. I went back to the State Department.

The Final Years

At first I joined the State Department Task Force on the disintegrating Soviet Union. It was an eye-opener. With the exception of a few large cities where diplomats were not allowed to leave, the Soviet Union was by all standards a third world country. A substantial portion of the population had no running water, sewer systems or paved roads. The Soviets had poured almost all the funds into weapons and propaganda. Now the Soviet Union had broken down into a dozen different countries. Under a tightly controlled economy we identified over 5,000 consumer items produced in only one factory. Simple items, like kitchen matches, were produced in only one place. If that factory now wanted to sell their products to the other former Soviet countries, they demanded hard currencies. Most did not have this.

A serious public health issue arose when it was discovered that almost all vaccines used in the Soviet Union were produced in Bulgaria. Demanding hard currency, they were no longer sending vaccines to be used to vaccinate an enormous number of children. Some other discoveries would have been amusing if they were not so serious. A number of electrical power plants closed down leaving thousands without power. They were no longer receiving coal for fuel. The coals mines closed because they did not have timber to shore up the tunnels. The timber suppliers closed down because they no longer had power!!

All this was interesting but not a permanent assignment. I searched around for something without the usual stress and long hours until I found the ideal spot. I joined the Foreign Service Grievance Board as a State Department representative. The Grievance Board was the final court of appeal for employees of State, AID, CIA, Peace Corps and a handful of smaller agencies.

All of the grievances we handled were interesting but it is inappropriate to discuss them individually. About half the time the agencies lost their case for not following their own regulations. The other half of the time – with a few glaring exceptions – the employees lost for not following the same regulations. Usually the case revolved around money. Employees had collected often substantial amounts of funds and then balked at having to repay them. A common example would be an employee who collected a large travel advance to move from one overseas post to another. The family might take a circuitous route, enjoy a nice vacation and spend extra time on the trip. All of this is acceptable but not on the government's money. When asked to refund a large portion of their travel advance for the time and places not on a direct route, they would file a grievance. They usually lost.

In September 1994 I quit working under a program that allowed employees three months to relocated while on full salary. We moved to Arizona and I officially retired on January 1, 1995.

Afterthoughts

In the course of my career I have been shot at in Viet-Nam, Colombia and Peru. I've faced two serious assignation attempts. I have been involved in some manner with wars in Viet-Nam, Colombia, Chad, Ethiopia and Peru. I have contracted hepatitis, amoebic dysentery, malaria and a host of never identified diseases. I have been sprayed with Agent Orange and given an office with open 55 gallon drums of DDT powder. I've lost hearing from artillery firings and jet helicopters. The US Army has recognized my work for and with them. And yet, I cannot be buried in a National Cemetery.

I marvel that I have such an extraordinary family on many levels and yet we are so very ordinary on the level that counts. I hope that each one of them always knows that I have, do and will love them forever in spite of any adversity that comes.

No life can be lived on a few hundred pages and yet I do not wish to become simply a name on a family history. I know little of my ancestors and my children know even less of their biological ancestors. I hope that far down the line some descendant of ours will wonder who I was and will have some small idea. I was here and I did these things.

Appendix

As mentioned earlier my staff of Chinese employees in Hong Kong was composed of university graduates from Canada and the United States. Any second language is fraught with pitfalls. These people were dedicated and intelligent but still, stuff happens. Here are a few collected examples from their files complied and handed to me. The purpose of their efforts was to filter out refugees that I knew without an interview would not be eligible.

Medical conditions

"...wounded in the front leg."

"...stepped on a mine and received a medical discharge."

"Baby covered with scabs and skin disease; has beautiful round eyeballs." (Always be positive!

"This child is mentally retarded – Healthy and bright."

"She is eight months pregnant. Enjoys baseball, long jump and high jump."

"...paralyzed in lower abdomen."

"This fanny is basically illiterate" (I think he meant 'family.')

Professional qualifications (Explanations below)

"Screws thermos bottles" *(Before you throw out your thermos, remember that he simply placed on the top as it came down the assembly line.)*

"Crane lifter"

"Making watches bend"

"Fogman"

"Shipping local staff"

"Sells girls"

"Building cleaning ladies"

"Motorcycle repair/ballet dancer"

"Secretary guard"

"Owner of a wreck shop"
"Ladder polisher"

"Works in a fartory"

"Wanton noodle maker"

"(before '75) Stud, (after '75) Mother's helper" *("Stud" was short for student.)*

"Tricycle rider" *(Meaning those three wheeled taxis common in Asia.)*

"Fishing net knitter"

"Running shoe maker"

"Ass inspector for police" (*Ah, those punctuation marks do count*)

Interesting observations

"Applicant laid a number of times during interview." (*And probably didn't tell the truth about it.*)

"Likes breeding poultry – young and innocent" (*She or the poultry?*)

"He is illitered" (*Look who's talking.*)

"Dang Thang – rubber factory worker – no children" (*No surprise here.*)

"Became a road mender at 15 and reared pigs." (*Hey, slow down!*)

And last, but not least, "Arrested for illegal erection on unleased property."

As mentioned earlier in the book, I sometimes had to advise refugees to change their names. Here are a few of the people that received this advice. In Vietnamese, the pronunciation was nothing like it would be in English, but they were going to be dealing with English speakers. How would you pronounce these?

Dam Yu

Tu Tu

Ha Chieu

On The Lam

Nguyen van Loc AKA Herry Peter

Mai Thi Dong

Tru Le Hung

Tieng Le Dong

Ho Mo

And the Grand Prize Winner – "Le Phat Phuc – accepted by France"

Postscript

Hazel and I have now been married for 34 years and retired in Arizona after tours together in the Philippines, Chad, Peru and Washington. We still travel as often as money allows.

My father died in 2000, followed by my mother a year later.

All of our children have worked hard for their success and deserve full credit. However, for Allan it was a far greater challenge because of his early educational deficits. Allan worked harder in school than any person I've known. With each year the huge gap in all those missing school years diminished and he graduated from high school with acceptable grades. He was absolutely determined to go to university in spite of overall grades that did not meet the standards. He applied in many places while refusing to play the affirmative action card. As he put it, *"I want them to accept me, not what I am."* Although he did not have the qualifications required, Old Dominion University in Norfolk, Virginia, asked to see him based mostly on his unusual background of no elementary school and education in several top-notch international schools. After an interview, they gave him a provisional acceptance. With large doses of determination, tenacity, hard work with long hours and drive to succeed that characterizes Allan he received his degree. He worked for 20 years for several corporations before deciding to launch his own business which was successful. After 14 years of marriage and a son, he and his wife parted. He has a daughter from his second marriage, also ended.

James graduated from university with a degree in Spanish and lives in Virginia.

David graduated from university in the top of his class with a degree in Computer Science. Today he works quite successfully in the Atlanta in his field. His wife, Andrea, and David now have two daughters.

Andrew joined the Army shortly after graduating from high school with plans to attend university after his two year hitch was completed. Eventually he earned his on-line Bachelor's degree.

12964111R00174

Made in the
USA
Monee, IL